Literature Activities for Reluctant Readers

Intermediate
TCM-354

Written by John and Patty Carratello

Illustrated by Cheryl Buhler, Sue Fullam, and Blanca Apodaca

Teacher Created Materials, Inc.
P.O. Box 1214
Huntington Beach, CA 92647
© *1991 Teacher Created Materials, Inc.*
Made in U.S.A.
ISBN 1-55734-354-3

Table of Contents

Table of Contents *(cont.)*

Introduction

Do you know kids who just don't like to read? Such reluctant readers are easy to spot. When it's time to read, they're the ones who suddenly have to go the restroom or visit the school nurse. And while some of the more covert ones will just sit quietly, looking at pictures in a book, others may become disruptive and do their best to keep any reading in the classroom from happening at all—for themselves or anyone else.

The simple fact is NOT EVERYONE LIKES TO READ! As teachers and parents, however, we have the opportunity to help the reluctant reader find value in books.

In *Literature Activities for Reluctant Readers,* methods for reaching our less-than-enthusiastic readers are outlined. A selection of engaging books and activities to support each method are also suggested.

It is the hope that the ideas presented in this book will help turn reluctant readers into eager ones!

Teacher's Guide

Books are wonderful friends. They can introduce us to many new people and places. They can help us with our problems, and make us feel better about who we are. They are with us anytime we want them to be and can always be trusted to give us something interesting to do.

But for the reluctant reader, books are not friends. They are not a joy to touch, open, read, finish, and read again. Reluctant readers do not become absorbed in books or grow to treasure them. For some reason, the world of books and the entertainment and enlightenment books can offer is closed to them.

Not wanting to read is not a quality that is inborn in children. All babies like to touch and explore the world around them, and if that world contains colorful, appealing picture books, a child will naturally want to investigate their interesting pages. If books are read aloud to children from a very early age, they will know the possibilities of wonderful things that can be found between two covers. They will delight in exploring books on their own. No—reluctant readers are not born reluctant readers.

Relucant readers are made. Raised in a home where stimulating books are not easily accessible and reading from books is not frequently seen and heard, a child will not develop the desire for books that exists in a home enriched by books and reading. The lack of a stimulating book-aware home environment is one reason for the development of a reluctant reading habit.

Reluctant readers are made. Sometimes a child has difficulty mastering the decoding skills necessary to make reading easy. For these children, reading is a struggle and brings only discouragement and perhaps laughter from their peers. Not all children master word-recognition skills at the same time. It is wrong to make them feel inadequate in any way because they do not have a skill level that is the same as the level of more fluent readers. A true fluency with reading, and the ability to become absorbed in books, does not always come in second or third grade. So the best thing we can do for young readers is teach them to love books.

Reluctant readers are made. For some disinterested readers, their early school experiences were filled with books that were used only to teach concepts, rather than to spark curiosity and imaginative thinking. Books were perceived by them as dull—things to be suffered through only while in school. Books that caused them to think, to imagine, to laugh, to cry, to feel, to become the character, to enjoy completely, were not shown to or opened for them. These children have not experienced any pleasure from reading in the past, so why should their future with books be any different?

Teacher's Guide *(cont.)*

What can you do to help children grow to love books? Here are some ideas.

- One extremely important thing you can do to help your reluctant readers get hooked on reading is to be genuinely thrilled with books. Don't confine your interest in books only to reading time. Share books about many things throughout the day.

- Do your best to supply books for your students that relate to a subject in which they have a keen interest. Work with your students and their parents to determine areas of interest.

- At school and in the home, children must be surrounded by interesting books and interested readers. If a value is attached to books and reading, children will begin to wonder what they are missing if they do not read.

- Give children time to read books of their choice in class on a regular basis. During this time, you read a book of your choice, too!

- Try to connect books to other curricular areas whenever possible. Books make more sense if they become an integral part of a child's whole learning experience.

- Invite guest readers from your community. Kids like to know that others they know enjoy books. Start with the principal, or the owner of a place where kids like to go in their afterschool time.

- Read aloud with enthusiasm daily.

- Discuss what you read, not to test the kids on their ability to remember facts from the books, but to share ways to relate what's read to their own lives.

- Use cooperative learning strategies to engage your students. They will often feed off the excitement and ideas that can be generated in a group setting.

- Encourage students to write in a journal about what they've read and how they feel about it.

To help children overcome a feeling of continued failure with reading, individualize your instruction whenever possible, helping these students choose books at their interest and ability level. Remind them that it is all right to make mistakes, and that the reward of the enjoyment of books is worth the effort it takes to become a successful reader.

Teacher's Guide *(cont.)*

You can help reluctant readers become eager readers. *Literature Activities for Reluctant Readers* will give you some ideas about how to capture the excitement of books for each child in your class.

In addition to the Teacher's Guide you are reading now, this book contains a Parents' Guide. We all know the importance a home filled with the love of books has for nurturing readers. This guide can be sent home for the parents of your students to read and apply. Encourage parent support and feedback.

The remainder of the book follows this format:

1. A method for stimulating an interest in reading is introduced with a page that can be colored and used for display in a learning center. Fill the center with books related to the particular method described on this sheet.

2. These methods are each followed by a selection of engaging books and activities which support the method introduced.

Here is a list of some of the methods that can be used to reach kids and help them really want to read.

- Reading can be fun. It can even make you laugh!
- Reading can help you understand problems you might be having in your life.
- Reading can help you learn more about things that really interest you.
- Reading can take you to different times and different worlds.
- Reading can help you understand things in life that are sometimes hard to understand.
- Reading can hold your interest to the point that you become completely absorbed in what you read.
- Reading can open new ways of thinking for you.
- Reading can make you feel better about yourself.
- Reading can teach you how to do things you want to learn.
- Enjoying books by the same author or on the same subject makes you want to read more by that author or on that subject.
- Reading is a great way to use your time!

If a reluctant reader has a pleasurable experience with one book, the door is opened. He or she is on the way to becoming an eager reader, ready and willing to experience the pleasure of reading again. And you can help!

Parents' Guide

You, as parents, hold the key to the world of reading for your child. If you show genuine interest in books, read for pleasure with your child and in view of your child, and encourage your child's interest in books with trips to the library or the bookstore, your child will be a reflection of the value you place on books and reading.

You can help your child select books that he or she will enjoy. Work together to complete this Interest Inventory. Then search for books that match your child's interest and ability level. Be sure to share what you have found with your child's teacher. The teacher will want to help, too!

INTEREST INVENTORY

Name: _____

Here are some things I would like to learn more about:

country: _____	music: _____
sport: _____	mammal: _____
spider: _____	invention: _____
holiday: _____	planet: _____
time in history: _____	custom: _____
bird: _____	food: _____
plant: _____	weather: _____
hobby: _____	reptile: _____
machine: _____	career: _____
car: _____	person: _____
disease: _____	insect: _____
place: _____	other: _____

On the next page, you will find some suggestions to help nurture a love of reading in your home. If you're already doing them, continue to do so. If you find some new ideas here that sound interesting, try them. You'll be helping your child become a lifelong reader!

Parent's Guide
"Helping Your Child To Read"

1. Set a good example. Read for pleasure and show and share that pleasure.

2. Leave interesting books lying around. Encourage your child to handle books frequently, carefully, and respectfully.

3. Read aloud eagerly to your child. Show him or her how much you enjoy this reading time. Make it special and do it each night if possible!

4. Provide a good reading light for your child's bed area. Encourage a relaxing nightly reading period. Give your child a special hug as you turn off the light at bedtime.

5. Be tuned in to what interests your child. Find books and other reading material in these areas of interest.

6. Discuss books and current events as a family.

7. Ask your child to read to you. Don't be anxious or impatient with his or her reading ability. Listen to the child read; do not listen for reading mistakes.

8. Encourage your child to share what he or she has read in books. Discuss stories, plots, characters, conflicts, resolutions, and feelings.

9. Visit the library together. Be sure your child has a library card and encourage its use. Use yours, too!

10. Share a reading interest. Both of you read books on the same subject and share what you've learned.

11. Be pleased with your child's reading progress. Give specific and genuine praise.

12. Let your child select books he or she wants to own. You and other family members and friends could give these books as gifts on special occasions or as reading rewards. Encourage your child to purchase books using his or her own money, too! Books a child has selected to own are friends for a long, long time!

DO YOU LIKE TO LAUGH?

READ ONE OF THESE BOOKS AND ENJOY YOURSELF!

Skinnybones

by Barbara Park

Alex "Skinnybones" Frankovitch likes to make people laugh. He learned that about himself in kindergarten when he sneezed Peter Donnelly's fuzz collection all over the room—on purpose. His classmates' appreciation of his humor was so great, Alex decided to keep up the clowning. That, and baseball. Even though Alex is the worst player on the team, and has been for six years, year after year he plays. And this year, he plays head to head with Little League's super hero—T.J. Stoner.

Alex often uses his wisecracking to draw attention to himself and, as a result, his big mouth gets him into difficult situations, especially with T.J. Stoner.

Skinnybones is a book kids will identify with and love!

"Oh, Alex, the things you say and do!"

Alex Frankovitch, also known as Skinnybones, loves to wisecrack. He absolutely **loves** to make people laugh.

On the cards below are different situations that happened in the book. Cut the cards apart and stack them in a deck. In groups of three or four, deal out the cards equally. Each player takes a turn, acting out or describing what Alex does to be funny in the situation written on one of the cards he or she is holding. Continue the game until the group has finished all its cards.

1. Alex dumps ten pounds of cat food on the kitchen floor to search for a contest entry form that was inside the bag.	2. Alex holds Peter Donnelly's fuzz collection in kindergarten.	3. Alex makes a strong impression with his new teacher, Miss Henderson, on the first day of fifth grade.	4. Alex is handed the microphone after receiving the Most Improved Player Trophy for the sixth baseball season in a row.
5. Alex hears that a member of his baseball team is planning to bunt.	6. T.J. grabs Alex's shirt and pulls Alex's face right up to his.	7. Alex doesn't want to play in the baseball game against T.J.'s team.	8. Alex doesn't want to be a sheep in the school Christmas play.
9. Alex hits one of T.J.'s pitches and runs to first base.	10. Harold Marshall gets up, ready to tease Alex as he walks by his desk to sharpen his pencil.	11. Alex is asked who his favorite relative is.	12. Alex adds a little something special of his own to songs in church.

"Oh, Alex, the things you say and do!" (cont.)

As readers of *Skinnybones,* we expect the things Alex Frankovitch says and does to be very, very funny. When he needs to talk himself out of or into a particular situation, we know we can count on some pretty creative storytelling.

What do you think Alex might say or do in each of the following situations? Work with a partner if you'd like. Choose one or more of your situations to perform for the class.

> You have forgotten to do your homework three times this week. What are your excuses?

> The P.E. teacher has decided to take your suggestion of a square dance team seriously. But first, you must outline the team's practices, uniforms, competitions, and coaching responsibilities. The team's future depends on you.

> T.J. Stoner has decided he now wants to be your friend.

> You have finally been asked for your autograph!

> You decide to go out for baseball for the seventh year in a row. Your coach sees you coming.

> Your seventh grade teacher, who is new to your school and your town and knows nothing about you, asks you to introduce yourself to the class.

> The Kitty Fritters people **do** want you to dress up like a Kitty Fritter and dance around a cat dish for the T.V. commercial.

> Your mother and father want to talk to you about your wisecracking in school.

> You have been asked to run for Class President. Your opponent is none other than T.J. Stoner.

And You?

How do **you** feel about Alex Frankovitch?

THE ALEX FRANKOVITCH QUESTIONNAIRE

1. Do you like Alex Frankovitch? Explain your answer.

_____

_____

_____

2. How would you react to Alex Frankovitch if you were:

his best friend? _____

_____

his baseball coach? _____

_____

his teacher? _____

_____

his mother? _____

_____

his father? _____

_____

his fish? _____

_____

3. Would you like Alex Frankovitch:

as your friend? _____

_____

in your class? (You're a student, too.) _____

_____

on your baseball team? _____

_____

4. How like Alex Frankovitch are you? Circle your response.

| exactly like him, ALWAYS! | more like him than not like him | like him when I want to be, but I know when to stop | more not like him than like him | not like him at all, EVER! |

How To Eat Fried Worms

by Thomas Rockwell

Alan bets Billy fifty dollars that he can't eat fifteen worms. Well, fifty dollars is a lot of money for a boy Billy's age. Fifty dollars can buy Billy that used minibike he wants. So Billy takes the bet!

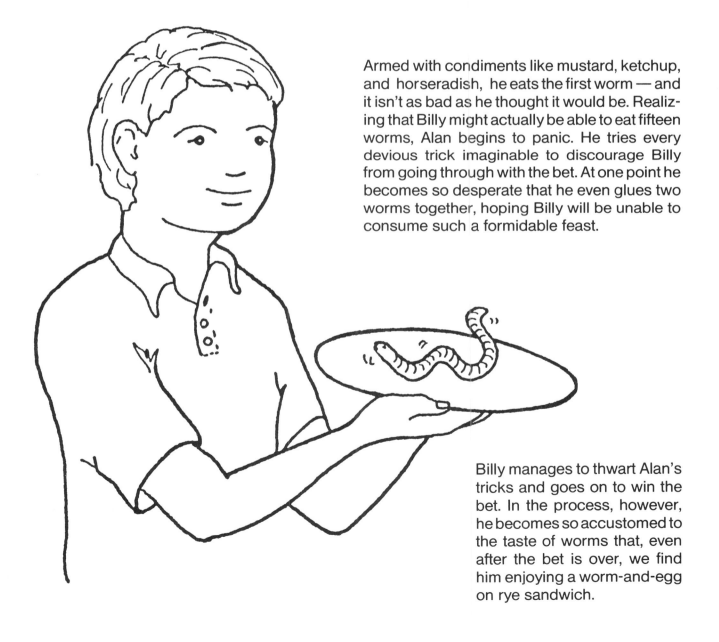

Armed with condiments like mustard, ketchup, and horseradish, he eats the first worm — and it isn't as bad as he thought it would be. Realizing that Billy might actually be able to eat fifteen worms, Alan begins to panic. He tries every devious trick imaginable to discourage Billy from going through with the bet. At one point he becomes so desperate that he even glues two worms together, hoping Billy will be unable to consume such a formidable feast.

Billy manages to thwart Alan's tricks and goes on to win the bet. In the process, however, he becomes so accustomed to the taste of worms that, even after the bet is over, we find him enjoying a worm-and-egg on rye sandwich.

Our Favorite Recipes

For many people, nearly any type of food can be eaten if the recipe is right. During her "referee" time, Billy's mother tries her best to make his worms palatable.

Here is Mrs. Forrester's first try.

ALSATIAN SMOTHERED WORM

* Dredge the worm with seasoned flour.

* Saute in three tablespoons drippings until browned.

* Cover with sliced onions, pour over one cup thick sour cream, cover pot closely, and bake in a slow oven until tender.

Mrs. Forrester also made Billy another worm recipe. Based on the description given in the book, create a recipe for "Whizbang Worm Delight."

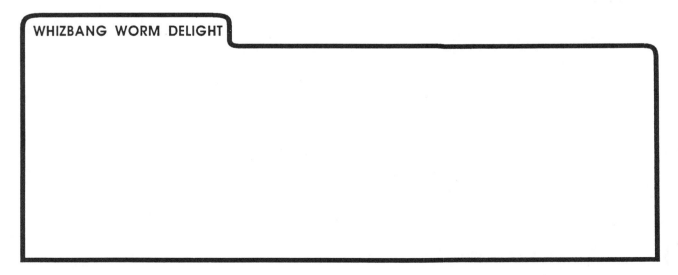

WHIZBANG WORM DELIGHT

Do you think **your** mother or father would help you eat worms by creating interesting ways to eat them?

Could **you** think of recipes that might make worms taste appealing? Work in groups to write worm recipes. Use the recipe card on the next page to record your creation!

Our Favorite Recipes

Work in groups to write interesting worm recipes. Use cookbooks for ideas and procedures. Complete a recipe card for each creation.

Name of recipe: _____

_____

Created by: _____

_____

Directions:

When you have finished, compile your recipes into a class cookbook. Try some of the recipes, **using spaghetti instead of worms.**

     17   *TCM-354 Literature Activities for Reluctant Readers*

Could You Swallow It?

Billy is able to eat fifteen worms in order to win a bet with his friend Alan. He even develops a liking for their taste!

Describe how you feel about worms.

_____

_____

_____

_____

_____

Could you eat fifteen worms to win a

bet? _____

_____

_____

_____

Would you bet a friend that he or she could not eat fifteen worms? _____

Why? _____

_____

Would you encourage a friend to eat fifteen worms to win a bet? _____ What would you say?

_____

_____

Would you discourage a friend from eating fifteen worms to win a bet? _____ What would you say?

_____

_____

Do you think if you ate fifteen worms, you might begin to enjoy the taste as Billy did? Why?

_____

_____

_____

18

Could You Swallow It?

*   Make a list of ten foods you would not be likely to eat. You may include worms as one of your choices. Put a star next to the three things you dislike most on your list.

TEN FOODS I WOULD NOT BE LIKELY TO **SWALLOW**

1 _____   6 _____

2 _____   7 _____

3 _____   8 _____

4 _____   9 _____

5 _____   10 _____

---

*   Trade your paper with another student in class. Circle three items on your classmate's list that you would be least likely to want to swallow.

*   Trade papers back. You now have your own paper.

*   Report the starred and circled items to your teacher. He or she will write these choices on the board, eliminating any duplications from other classmates.

*   Choose the three most "unswallowable" things from the class list. Write them on this ballot form.

*   Cut the ballot from this paper and give it to your teacher. Your teacher will record the ballot votes on the board and determine what is the most "unswallowable" choice of your class.

"COULD YOU SWALLOW IT?" **BALLOT**

These are three foods I would be least likely to swallow:

1. The **absolute** worst:

_____

2. Almost the worst:

_____

3. A little better, but still disgusting:

_____

Where the Sidewalk Ends

by Shel Silverstein

Welcome to a world where everything is possible—a world we're invited to view **if** we are dreamers and pretenders or anyone else who thinks imaginatively—a world where the sidewalk, and all else that may be predictable, ends.

Shel Silvertein creates an amazing variety of poetry for *Where the Sidewalk Ends* that touches different parts of who we are. There is a poem for everyone in this book. Sometimes we can identify with the situation of the narrator of a poem, and sometimes revel in the absurdity of others. Above all, Shel Silverstein helps us get in touch with the fun and feeling poetry can bring.

So, take a step. Follow the children's chalk-white arrows to the place where the sidewalk ends. You'll be glad you did!

Humorous Choices

Many of the poems Shel Silverstein includes in *Where the Sidewalk Ends* are very humorous.

What is it about this poetry that makes people want to laugh? With the help of a partner, choose one of the poems in the box and determine just what it is that makes the poem so funny. Then practice reading your poem in such a way that you accent that humor.

"I Must Remember"

"The Loser"

"Smart"

"I'm Making a List"

"Sick"

"Ridiculous Rose"

"The Crocodile's Toothache"

"Sarah Cynthia Sylvia Stout
  Would Not Take the Garbage Out"

"Hat"

"My Rules"

"Warning"

"The Edge of the World"

"The Dirtiest Man in
  the World"

"Eighteen Flavors"

"With His Mouth Full of Food"

"The Bagpipe Who Didn't
  Say No"

"Dreadful"

"Hungry Mungry"

When all the students in your class have finished practicing their selections, put on a "Comedy Hour!" During this hour, pairs will perform their poems for the class.

TCM-354 Literature Activities for Reluctant Readers

A Poem About . . .

Shel Silverstein writes about many different things in *Where the Sidewalk Ends.*

Try to write one or more poems about the subjects in the box below. When you have finished, read what Shel Silverstein has written about the same subject. Then decide which poem you like better, yours or his!

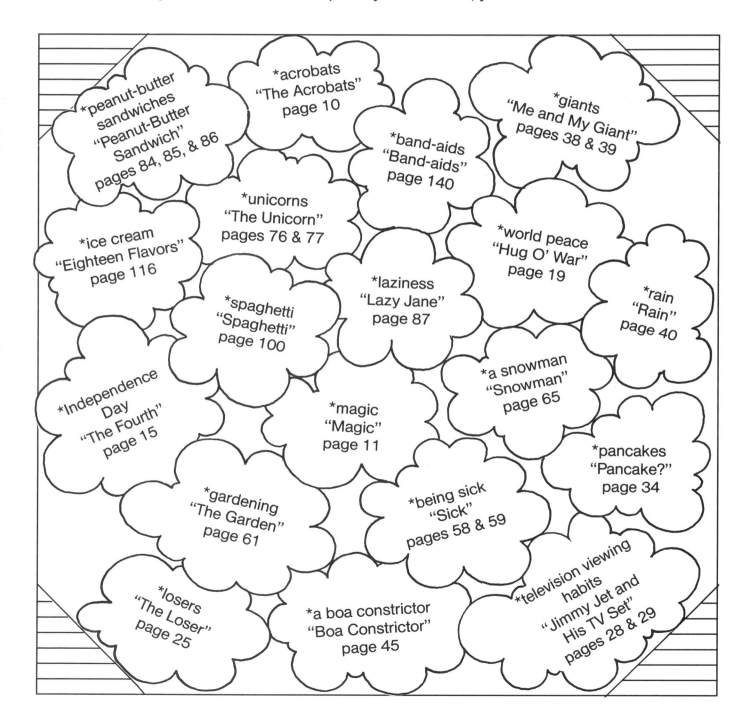

Reading Record

Books That Made Me Laugh

Keep a record of the books you read that **really** make you laugh. Explain why you find each book funny. Then trade lists with a friend and laugh some more!

Book: _____

Author: _____

Why it was funny: _____

_____

_____

Book: _____

Author: _____

Why it was funny: _____

_____

_____

Book: _____

Author: _____

Why it was funny: _____

_____

_____

Book: _____

Author: _____

Why it was funny: _____

_____

_____

PROBLEMS, PROBLEMS, PROBLEMS.

WE ALL HAVE PROBLEMS. SOMETIMES BOOKS CAN HELP!

Lila on the Landing

by Sue Alexander

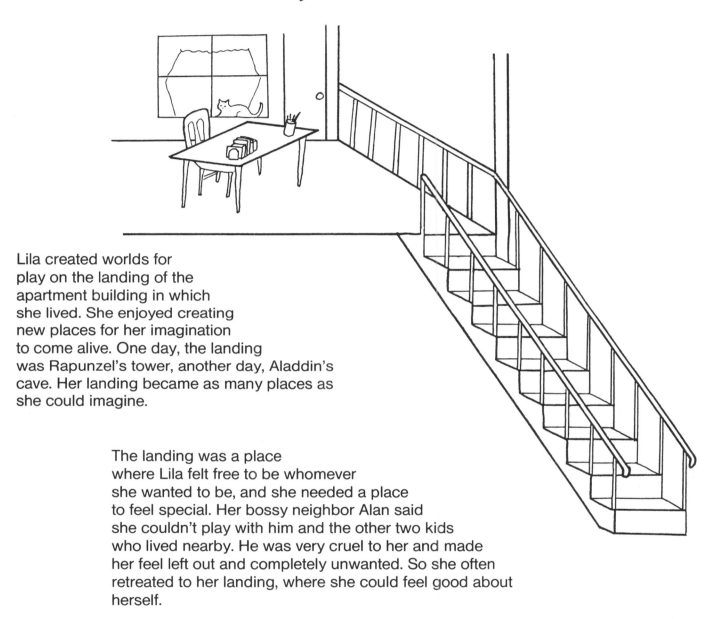

Lila created worlds for
play on the landing of the
apartment building in which
she lived. She enjoyed creating
new places for her imagination
to come alive. One day, the landing
was Rapunzel's tower, another day, Aladdin's
cave. Her landing became as many places as
she could imagine.

The landing was a place
where Lila felt free to be whomever
she wanted to be, and she needed a place
to feel special. Her bossy neighbor Alan said
she couldn't play with him and the other two kids
who lived nearby. He was very cruel to her and made
her feel left out and completely unwanted. So she often
retreated to her landing, where she could feel good about
herself.

But one day, her landing play attracted the other two kids away from Alan. They became fascinated by Lila's imaginative ideas and eagerly joined her. When Alan came up to the landing to get the other kids to play, Lila thought she would be left alone again. Much to her surprise, Jon and Amy stayed and left it up to Lila whether or not to include Alan in their landing project. She was tempted to hurt Alan the way he had hurt her so many times before, but she did not. She invited him to stay, and, with the invitation, showed her compassion and gained a friend.

Left Out

Alan made Lila feel left out, excluding her from playing with the others with such comments as, "you always drop the ball," "you always fall down," and "you don't get a turn." He succeeded in making Lila feel miserable.

Do you know how it feels to be left out?

---

* Has an older brother or sister told you to "get lost" because you were too little?

* Have adults left you out of conversations because they felt you wouldn't understand?

* Have you ever waited nearly to the end to be chosen because the choosers didn't think you were good enough?

* Did a teacher ever praise others in class for their work and neglect to mention yours, even though you worked as hard as you could?

* Have the neighborhood kids passed by your house on their way to play and forgotten to invite you to join them?

* Has one of your parents given more attention to someone else in the family than to you?

Explain your feelings about being left out on the back of this paper.

---

* Have you ever made someone else feel left out?

    Who? _____

    How? _____

    Why? _____

    _____

* Have you ever watched while someone was making another person feel left

    out? What did you do? _____

    _____

    _____

Explain your feelings about leaving people out on the back of this paper.

It's In Your Head!

Lila's landing is a magical place. It can be any world she can imagine. It has been Heidi's hut, Rapunzel's tower, and Aladdin's cave. It has been a restaurant, a television studio, a ship, a library, a stage, and a newspaper office.

> "I don't know what there is about the landing that makes me feel good inside, but it does ... Maybe it's that it can be any place that I want it to be."

Do you have (or have you ever had) a place like Lila's landing, a place where your imagination can just run wild? _____
If so, describe it.

_____

_____

_____

Find a place in your home, yard, or neighborhood that could be a place like Lila's landing.

Where is it? _____

_____

_____

_____

Could you go there every day? _____

_____

Would you be able to use this place for imaginative play? _____

_____

_____

_____

Who would you want to join you there?

_____

_____

_____

PLAN YOUR FIRST DAY THERE. USE PAGES 28 and 29 TO HELP YOU.

It's In Your Head!

Now that you have found a place like Lila's landing, it's time to plan your activities there.

*   Choose an activity that would be fun.

    What do you like to do?
    When you pretend, what do you pretend to be?
    What are some things you already know a lot about?
    What are some things you would love to learn more about?
    What careers interest you?
    What things are fun for you to do?

*   Decide on the props you will need
    to make your imaginative play
    area look realistic.

    You can make your props
    or gather together suitable
    props from your home and
    neighborhood.

*   Plan an appropriate costume.

    Your costume doesn't
    have to be elaborate,
    it just needs to be
    suited to your activity.

*   Decide on the activity that will
    be going on in your "landing" area.

    Many activities are possible for
    the themes you choose. For example, if
    you have decided to make an amusement
    park, you may choose to juggle, have a
    ring toss, give wagon rides, make balloon
    figures, ask your dog to do tricks,
    or sell popcorn!

*   Play as long as it is interesting and fun!

    Some activities may be great for just one day. Others may go on for a week!

TIME TO WARM UP! Practice planning props, costumes, and activities for each of these ideas Lila had for her landing: Aladdin's cave, Rapunzel's tower, a television studio, a ship, and a magic show. BRAINSTORM AS A CLASS! COME UP WITH AS MANY IDEAS AS POSSIBLE!

It's In Your Head! (cont.)

Work in groups of three or four. Brainstorm for a list of ten activities that would be fun to do.

TEN GREAT ACTIVITIES FOR OUR "LANDING"	
1 _____	6 _____
2 _____	7 _____
3 _____	8 _____
4 _____	9 _____
5 _____	10 _____

In your groups, complete a planning guide for one or more of your activities.

"LANDING" ACTIVITY PLANNING GUIDE	
Activity	
Props Needed	
Costume Design	
Theme-related Activities	
Additional Notes	

Now, try it! Have a great time imagining! Invite some friends, too!

Be a Perfect Person in Just Three Days!

by Stephen Manes

Milo Crinkley only wanted one thing in life—to be a perfect person. Then, one day while in the library looking for a monster story to read, a book fell off the shelf and hit him on the head. He read the title—*Be a Perfect Person in Just Three Days!*

From that moment on, Milo found it impossible to put the book down, even though the author, Dr. K. Pinkerton Silverfish, had his readers do some pretty strange things. In his quest for perfection, Milo agreed to do things like wear a necklace made of broccoli, go without eating for 24 hours, and finally, do absolutely nothing for another 24 hours (except for going to the bathroom and sipping weak tea slowly). These, of course, were things that inspired ridicule and questioning from nearly everyone.

In the end, Milo came to the conclusion that being a perfect person was not all that he thought it would be. Being perfect, he decided, was boring and no fun. Dr. Silverfish could have told him that on page 1, but Milo just had to find it out for himself!

Perfection!

Before reading *Be a Perfect Person in Just Three Days!*, work to create your own plan to achieve perfection.

My personal plan for perfection

by _____

Step 1: _____

_____

Step 2: _____

_____

Step 3: _____

_____

Step 4: _____

_____

Step 5: _____

_____

Any additional steps necessary for perfection have been listed on the back of this paper.

Good habits I should keep:	Bad habits I should break:

When you have finished your personal plan for perfection, join a small group. Come to a concensus on at least five ways to achieve perfection. Write your ideas neatly on a large piece of paper and display them for your class. Do your other classmates agree with your group's ideas? Do you agree with their ideas?

Perfection and Reality

On this page you will find two situations which will need some action taken as soon as possible. Look at each situation carefully.

On the next page create the perfect **and** the realistic solution for each problem.

Perfection and Reality

Create the perfect and the realistic solutions for each of the situations found on page 32.

In My Room . . .	
Perfection	**Reality**

Please Try Harder.	
Perfection	**Reality**

The War with Grandpa

by Robert Kimmel Smith

There is no place more comfortable for Peter Stokes than his bedroom. After all, he has lived in it the entire ten years of his life. So when he hears the news that he must give up his beloved room to his grandfather who is moving in with his family, Peter is furious!

Peter decides to take drastic action to show his grandpa how much his room means to him. He declares war, and his battle plans include some sneaky tricks. But Grandpa retaliates in grand style.

Both grandfather and grandson learn how much they mean to each other during times of war and times of peace. And because of their love, they are able to find a satisfying resolution for their conflict.

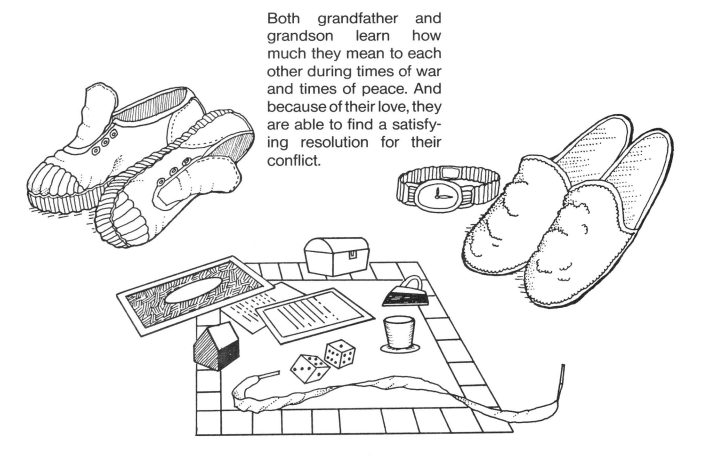

What Do You Mean?

In *The War with Grandpa,* Peter and Grandpa both have some things to say that are worth thinking about. Read these quotes and think about them. Then, complete the activity suggested for each of them.

"Grandpa had no life at all. Could you die from being sad? I wondered. Could you?"

-Peter

- Make it a point to communicate on a **regular** basis with your older relatives. Write letters, make phone calls, send pictures, and visit whenever possible.

- Try to brighten the days of some of your older neighbors who may live alone. Rake their leaves, draw pictures for them, bake cookies with them, just sit and talk. You'll help.

"War hurts. War wounds and kills and causes misery. Only a fool wants war."

- Grandpa

- Create a collage of newspaper clippings, magazine articles, and pictures to support this quote.

- Arrange what you collect about the misery of war in a bulletin board display.

A Plan for Peace

According to Peter and Grandpa, there are several causes of war. Wars are about taking over territory that belongs to others and about getting back what is yours. They are about power and greed. Wars are also about defending yourself and sticking up for your rights.

Peter gives this insight as to how wars get started and continue on:
"Your enemy does something bad to you, so you do something worse to him. Then he gets you back and you get him back and the whole thing gets bigger and bigger and meaner and meaner and in the end someone drops a bomb."

Grandpa gives Peter this advice:
"There are lots of ways of settling arguments without going to war. Peaceful ways."

On the next page, you will find five problems. Read each problem carefully. Decide on an action for each problem that would help to promote a war. Then anticipate what the reaction to your warlike action would be.

Now, decide on an action for the same problem that would promote peace. Then anticipate what the reaction to your peaceful action would be.

Share your ideas with the class.

A PLAN FOR PEACE

PROBLEM	WARLIKE ACTION	WARLIKE REACTION	PEACEFUL ACTION	PEACEFUL REACTION
A new kid in your school takes your place on the team. You still get to play, but not the same position.				
A kid in school begins to call you names that are not very nice.				
Your parents tell you that you will have to share your room with your younger brother or sister.				
Your best friend begins to spend more time with another kid in your grade than with you.				
There is a brand new, fascinating book in your classroom. You and another kid both want to take it home.				

Collecting Books About Problems

Pre-Activity Exercise

1. Explain to students that everyone has to face problems in his or her life. We sometimes have problems at home, at school, with friends, or even with ourselves.

2. Give students 5 minutes in their groups to list as many problems as they can that people their ages have.

3. After the 5 minutes are up, have groups take turns contributing to a class list that you compile on the board.

4. Have students help you consolidate problems that are similar.

CLASS ACTIVITY

Explain that sometimes the characters in books face the same kinds of problems that people face in real life, and that reading these books may help with those problems.

Announce a Scavenger Hunt! Give students a time limit of about 3 or 4 weeks to find as many books as they can that deal with problems faced by people their age. They may get help from librarians, teachers, parents, friends, or other people who may know of such books. For each book they find, students should fill out a 3"x5" index card according to the model below.

When a card has been completed, it may be pinned to a classroom bulletin board or placed in an indexed card file for student use throughout the year.

You may want to set a class goal to be achieved within the time allotted for the hunt. You may also want to find some way of acknowledging your students' efforts in meeting that goal.

BOOK: _____

AUTHOR: _____

PROBLEM AREA:

_____

_____

_____

SO YOU'VE FOUND SOMETHING YOU ARE INTERESTED IN? READ MORE ABOUT IT!

The Magic School Bus Inside the Earth

by Joanna Cole

For some people, reading about the geology of the Earth does not rank high on their list of book choices. However, these readers are in for quite a surprise when they board the magic school bus with an extraordinary teacher named Ms. Frizzle!

She is a teacher who truly believes in the concept of "hands-on" science. Ms. Frizzle takes her class inside the Earth to learn about it!

And learn about it is just what they do, as will those who read this very entertaining book. In fact, even kids who don't like reading about science, will look forward to another ride on the magic school bus, eager to learn more from this very **unusual** teacher!

Earth Science with Ms. Frizzle

Compile a study guide of the facts about the Earth Science you learned from Ms. Frizzle and her students.

MS. FRIZZLE'S EARTH SCIENCE FACTS
Where do rocks come from?
What are rocks made of?
What is soil?
How are rock layers formed?
Define the following words: sandstone _____ shale _____ limestone _____ fossil _____ stalagmite _____ _____ stalactite _____ _____ marble _____ slate _____ granite _____ volcano _____ _____ lava _____ pumice _____
Work as a class to create a rock collection. Label and display each rock neatly! See page 37 of *The Magic School Bus Inside the Earth* for ideas.

Earth Science with Ms. Frizzle (cont.)

Continue compiling your study guide of Earth Science facts.

> Label each of the parts that make up the crust of the Earth. Then complete the rock classification chart at the bottom of the page.

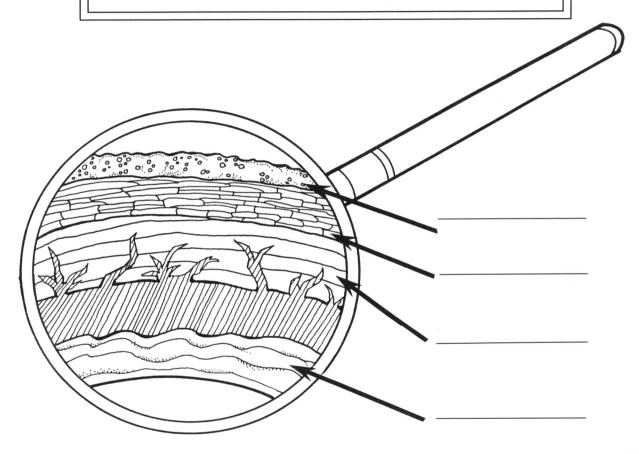

MS. FRIZZLE'S CRUST COMPOSITION CHART			
Part	Definition	Description	Example
Soil			
Sedimentary Rock			
Metamorphic Rock			
Igneous Rock			

Earth Science with Ms. Frizzle (cont.)

Continue compiling your study guide of Earth Science facts.

Label each of the parts that make up the inside of the Earth.

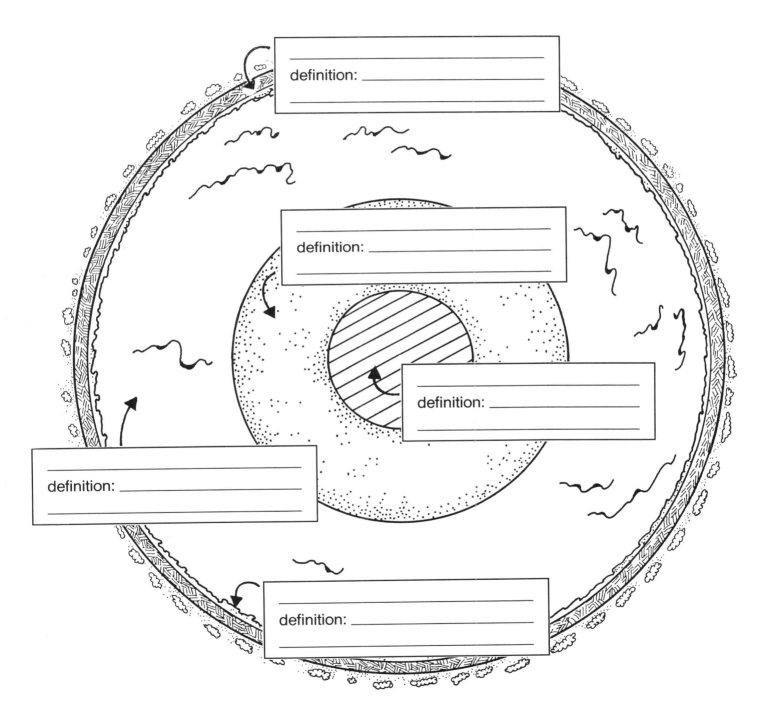

definition: _____

definition: _____

definition: _____

definition: _____

definition: _____

The Lesson

Create one page of a science lesson that Ms. Frizzle might present to her students. Choose the subject, design Ms. Frizzle's dress and shoes, decorate the room, explain a concept on the small notebook page, and write all the dialogue in the speech bubbles. Have fun, and share your lesson with the class!

Animal Fact/ Animal Fable

by Seymour Simon

Children are just naturally curious about animals. There are so many things about animals' lives and habits that are interesting, funny, amazing, or mysterious.

In *Animal Fact/Animal Fable,* Seymour Simon teaches his readers about twenty animals in a game-like format. He invites us to guess whether a statement on one page is a fact or a fable. We decide, then turn the page to find the answer.

Kids love this book. And perhaps after reading it, they will want to create their own fact and fable books about things that interest them!

Fact or Fable?

Before reading *Animal Fact/Animal Fable*, cut out the animal statement cards on this page. With tape or glue, attach them back to back with the answer cards found on page 47. Work with a partner to determine whether each animal statement is fact or fable. Write your answers on the flip side of each card. When you have finished, read Seymour Simon's book to check your answer cards!

Bats are blind.	Some bees only sting once.	An owl is a wise bird.	A turtle can walk out of its shell.
Some fish can climb trees.	Crickets tell the temperature with their chirps.	Elephants are afraid of mice.	Porcupines shoot their quills.
Dogs talk with their tails.	Ostriches hide their heads in the sand.	Goats will eat almost anything.	Bulls get angry when they see red.
Camels store water in their humps.	Snakes bite with their tongues.	Rats desert a sinking ship.	Raccoons wash their food.

Fact or Fable? (cont.)

Before reading *Animal Fact/Animal Fable*, cut out these "Fact or Fable" answer cards. With tape or glue, attach them back to back with the answer cards found on page 46. Work with a partner to determine whether each animal statement is fact or fable. Write your answers on the flip side of each card. When you have finished, read Seymour Simon's book to check your answer cards!

FACT or FABLE?	FACT or FABLE?	FACT or FABLE?	FACT or FABLE?
IDEAS:	IDEAS:	IDEAS:	IDEAS:
FACT or FABLE?	FACT or FABLE?	FACT or FABLE?	FACT or FABLE?
IDEAS:	IDEAS:	IDEAS:	IDEAS:
FACT or FABLE?	FACT or FABLE?	FACT or FABLE?	FACT or FABLE?
IDEAS:	IDEAS:	IDEAS:	IDEAS:
FACT or FABLE?	FACT or FABLE?	FACT or FABLE?	FACT or FABLE?
IDEAS:	IDEAS:	IDEAS:	IDEAS:

A Test for Friends

After you have finished reading *Animal Fact/Animal Fable,* design a test for your friends that is based on information you have learned from reading the book. You might want to ask such questions as these:

* "What fact did you already know before reading this book?"
* "How many lives do cats have?"
* "What fact or fable surprised you most?"

Have fun! Exchange tests with your classmates, too!

ANIMAL FACT AND FABLE TEST

created by _____

Amazing Poisonous Animals

by Alexandra Parsons

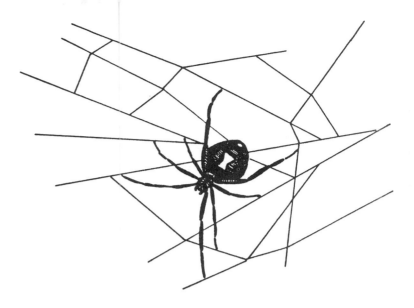

Drawn into the book by true-to-life pictures and informed by easily read text, readers of all ages will be fascinated by the creatures they encounter in *Amazing Poisonous Animals.*

The Gila monster chews its poison into its prey. A poisonous fish can still inject poison even after its death. The skin of the tiny, golden arrow-poison frog contains the most deadly poison that is made by an animal.

Facts like these, and pictures that bring each animal vividly to life, will make this book one that will be read again and again.

Where's the Poison?

The poison source is in a different place in each of these poisonous animals. Color each animal. Then cut it out and glue it to a card. On the back of each card write information about the animal, including the location of its poison source.

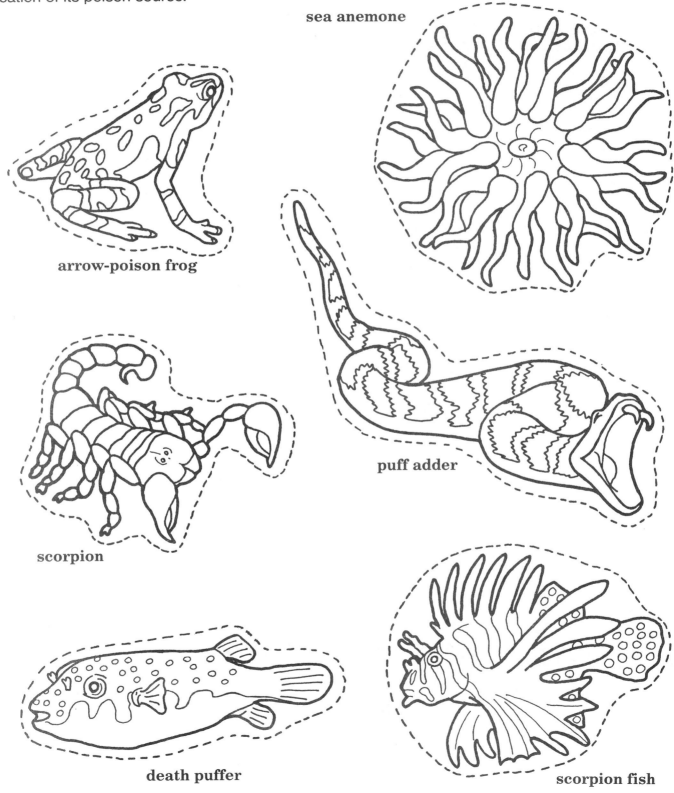

sea anemone

arrow-poison frog

scorpion

puff adder

death puffer

scorpion fish

Learn More About It!

Many fascinating animals and their habits are introduced in this book. Find out more about one or more of the animals on the list below. Then share your research with the class.

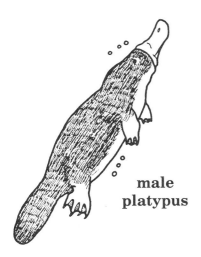

male platypus

* jellyfish
* imperial scorpion
* male platypus
* centipede
* cobra
* rattlesnake
* fire salamander
* red-spotted newt
* spiny newt
* California newt
* arrow-poison frog

blue-ringed octopus

* scorpion fish
* Australian stonefish
* stringray
* Gila monster
* beaded lizard
* wasp
* African puff adder
* sea anemone
* clown fish

wasp

* honeybee
* killer bee
* black widow
* giant toad
* *fugu*
* death puffer
* sea wasp
* blue-ringed octopus
* puffer fish
* Australian funnel-web

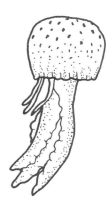

jellyfish

There are other poisonous animals that are not mentioned in *Amazing Poisonous Animals*. Prepare a report on one of them to share with your class. Be sure to include a color illustration of the animal in your report.

Read About Your Favorites!

What is your favorite:

subject in school? _____

hobby? _____

animal? _____

sport? _____

game? _____

historical period? _____

food? _____

place? _____

career? _____

Choose two favorites from the above list and find two or three books you can read about each of them. Write the book information here.

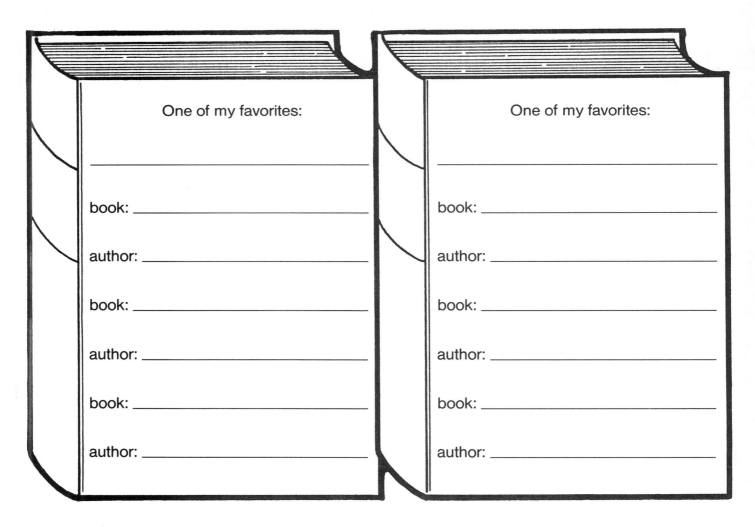

One of my favorites:

_____

book: _____

author: _____

book: _____

author: _____

book: _____

author: _____

One of my favorites:

_____

book: _____

author: _____

book: _____

author: _____

book: _____

author: _____

YOU *REALLY* LIKE THE WAY AN AUTHOR WRITES? THEN FIND *MORE* OF HIS OR HER BOOKS TO READ!

Cowardly Clyde

by Bill Peet

Clyde, the great war-horse, had the misfortune to be paired with the brave young knight, Sir Galavant. This knight was eager to battle any and every brute imaginable, much to Clyde's dismay. You see, Sir Galavant, who was brave as a man could be, rode upon a great war-horse who wasn't brave at all.

So when Sir Galavant rode off to conquer a terrible ox-footed ogre who had been terrorizing the farms and villages, Clyde was less than thrilled with the prospect of facing the fearsome beast. He pretended to be brave on the hunt for the ogre, but when he came face to face with its fierce owlish eyes, Clyde turned and fled the forest.

When the horse reached safety, he was horrified to find himself unridden. Sir Galavant was back in the forest with the ox-footed ogre. Mustering up all the courage he could, Clyde raced back to the forest, bit the beast on the tail, and led it away from his master, right into the bright sunlight. With one big "KER-PUFFLE!" the ogre exploded, unable to live without darkness and gloom.

Reunited with his fearless master, Clyde began to feel pretty brave himself. And no one could contest that—especially one "KER-PUFFLED!" ox-footed ogre.

Language That Will Grab You!

Bill Peet is a master of language. He knows how to choose just the right words for his characters and their situations.

Written below are a collection of sentences taken in part from **Cowardly Clyde.** The words that are **italicized** are not the words Bill Peet wrote. Work with a partner to find these sentences in the book. Then write the word or words Bill Peet used instead of the **italicized** parts.

1. "And when he heard the news that a **monster** was on the rampage far out in the countryside, the **horse** was **scared**." _____

2. "Don't lose your heads! I'll **get the monster!** I'll finish him off **quickly!**" _____

3. "But anyone who dared go in after him would be a **fool**!" _____

4. "Then pretty soon **they heard a noise** through the trees like the breathing of some gigantic thing." _____

5. "Then, to the horse's **surprise**, Sir Galavant shouted, **"Wake up!"** _____

6. **"Oh boy!"** he **said** when he **saw** the Knight on horseback, right under his **nose.**" _____

7. "Then **making brave noises,** Clyde went **back into the woods.**" _____

8. "He came **quickly** through the trees, gaining with every **step.**" _____

9. "In one last **try,** he made it out into the meadow and **pulled** the huge ogre out after him." _____

10. "He let go of the horse and **screamed.**" _____

On the back of this paper, discuss why Bill Peet's words work so well to tell a story.

The Cowardly and the Brave

Answer questions 1, 2, 3, and 4 before you read *Cowardly Clyde.* Complete the rest of the questionnaire after you have finished the story.

The Cowardly

1. Define what it means to be a coward. _____
    _____
    _____

2. Give an example of something a cowardly person would do. _____
    _____
    _____

3. How do you think the world views people who are cowardly? _____
    _____
    _____

4. Would you consider yourself to be cowardly? _____
    Give at least one good example to support your opinion.
    _____
    _____

    NOW READ *Cowardly Clyde.*

5. What makes Clyde cowardly? _____
    _____
    _____

6. Is he happy being a coward? Explain your answer.
    _____
    _____

7. On the back of this page, write a dialogue between Clyde and Sir Galavant in which Clyde confesses that he is a coward. Perform your dialogue with a partner.

8. How would this story be different if Clyde *stayed* cowardly? Write one page from this "new" story. Try your best to use Bill Peet's style as you write.

9. What is one good reason to be cowardly? _____
    _____

10. Do you think it is all right to be cowardly? Why? _____
    _____
    _____

The Cowardly and the Brave

Answer questions 1, 2, 3, and 4 before you read *Cowardly Clyde*. Complete the rest of the questionnaire after you have finished the story.

The BRAVE

1. Define what it means to be brave. _____
   _____
   _____

2. Give an example of something a brave person would do. _____
   _____
   _____

3. How do you think the world views people who are brave? _____
   _____
   _____

4. Would you consider yourself to be brave? _____
   Give at least one good example to support your opinion.
   _____
   _____

   NOW READ *Cowardly Clyde.*
5. What makes Sir Galavant brave? _____
   _____
   _____

6. What makes Clyde brave? _____
   _____
   _____

7. Is Clyde happier being cowardly or brave? Why? _____
   _____
   _____

8. On the back of this page, write a dialogue between Sir Galavant and Clyde in which Sir Galavant admits that being brave is not all that is said to be. Perform your dialogue with a partner for the class.

9. How would this story be different if Clyde was the brave one and Sir Galavant cowardly? Write one page from this "new" story. Try your best to use Bill Peet's style as your write.

10. If you could choose, would you rather be cowardly or brave? Explain your answer thoroughly. _____
    _____
    _____

Kermit the Hermit

by Bill Peet

Kermit the hermit is a rather greedy crab. He spends most of his time collecting and hoarding all sorts of unusable things in his rock cave.

But one day, a young boy saves Kermit from being buried in the sand by an angry dog. The crab vows to repay the boy someday.

And repay him Kermit does. While hiding from a shark in an old, old chest, he discovers he is sitting on piles of gold. Carefully, piece by piece, Kermit takes it from under the sea to his rock cave.

With the help of a friendly pelican, Kermit drops the gold into the chimney of the boy's house. Both the crab and the boy who saved him are happy.

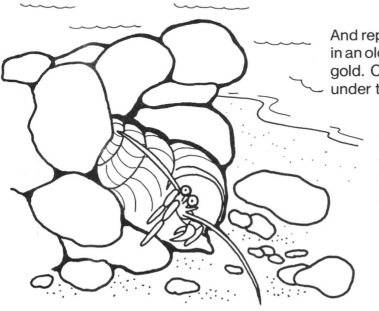

Peet's Poetry!

Bill Peet's story of Kermit is a delightful one, and would be even if it was told in simple prose. But Peet's use of poetry to tell the story makes *Kermit the Hermit* extraordinary! Not only is this story fun to read silently, it is hilarious to read aloud!

> There are 27 pages of rhyming poetry in this story. Assign each student a page of the story to practice reading aloud. If you have more students, divide some of the longer pages for two readers instead of one. After everyone has practiced, read the book aloud as a class. It's fun!

Add to your appreciation of the craftsmanship and humor with which Bill Peet created *Kermit the Hermit*. Search through the book to find the rhyming pair!

1. slow motion

_____

2. crab-hungry enemies

_____

3. survival

_____

4. tearing

_____

5. most sorrowful sigh

_____

6. amount

_____

7. altogether

_____

8. shark stayed without

_____

9. floppity flip

_____

10. scoop

_____

11. warm summer breeze

_____

12. bicycle

_____

Kermit the Hermit is a rhyming title. Try to think of some rhyming titles of your own! Share them with your class.

_____

_____

_____

Sea Creatures!

Bill Peet mentions several types of sea animals in *Kermit the Hermit.*

seagull	minnows	sardines
crab	halibut	herring
clams	blue shark	pelican

Work in small groups to research for facts about these sea creatures. Complete a **Sea Creature Profile** sheet (this page) and a **Sea Creature Habitat** sheet (page 61) for each of the above creatures.

SEA CREATURE PROFILE

sea animal: _____

description: _____

_____

_____

facts about its birth: _____

_____

life span: _____

food it eats: _____

_____

dangers it faces: _____

_____

special things it can do: _____

_____

_____

other interesting facts: _____

_____

Sea Creatures! (cont.)

Work in small groups to research for facts about the appearance and habitat of each of these sea creatures.

seagull	minnows	sardines
crab	halibut	herring
clams	blue shark	pelican

In the frame below, draw each of these animals accurately in the habitat that it is most commonly found. Be sure to use the appropriate colors.

* Make a book using all your profile and habitat sheets!

SEA CREATURE HABITAT

The Wump World

by Bill Peet

A peaceful world, filled with the pristine beauty of clear skies, sparkling water, and lush vegetation is the world of the Wumps. They live in harmony with nature and each other, content with their gentle lifestyle.

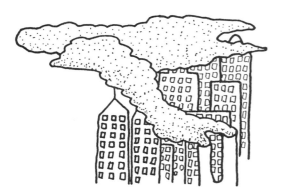

Without thought, their lovely world is changed—changed by industry-minded, environmentally unconscious invaders from another planet. The Wumps retreat underground as their world is changed above them. The changes bring high-rise buildings, freeway systems, and a world filled with pollution. It becomes so polluted that the selfish invaders decide to flee the planet to settle once again on an unpolluted world.

As the Wumps come above ground, they are greeted by a world more polluted than they could have imagined. However, amidst the ruin, they discover a small patch of their old world, and settle in to wait for the planet to renew itself.

What a Contrast!

The world of the Wumps and the world of the Pollutians were two strikingly different worlds. Contrast these worlds and their inhabitants in the chart below.

A CONTRAST OF TWO WORLDS	
The Wumps	The Pollutians
What their world is like:	What their world is like:
What the inhabitants are like:	What the inhabitants are like:

How does the place you live compare to each of these worlds?

On the back of this paper, prepare a chart that compares two very different places you have lived in or visited.

       TCM-354 Literature Activities for Reluctant Readers

A World for Wumps and Other Gentle Ones

Would you be able to design a world where Wumps and other gentle creatures could be happy? Work in small groups to plan your new world.

Here are some ideas to help you get started:

* Create a name for your world.

* Decide who will be allowed to live in this world. Be ready to support your inhabitant choices.

* Design a questionnaire that can be used to determine an applicant's worthiness for citizenship. (See page 65 for an example.)

* Establish rules of conduct that will be required of all inhabitants. (See page 66 for a form.)

* Make a flag that will be a powerful symbol for your world. Create a motto and creed, too.

* Write a national anthem that will serve to inspire the inhabitants to help your new world stay beautiful.

* Develop an illustrated list of the types of plants that would grow in your world.

* Design living quarters for the inhabitants.

* Plan a system of defense in case others who were not suitable invaded your world.

* Create a brochure to advertise the beauty and harmony of your world.

* Formulate an idea list that would help define your world. (See page 67 for an example.)

* Write a speech convincing the Wumps to come to your new world!

* Think of more ideas as a group!

The Wump World

QUESTIONNAIRE FOR CITIZENSHIP

Name of New World	

Applicant's name: Date:

Reason for citizenship application:

Answer the following questions completely and honestly.

1. Do you now, or have you ever, littered any environment in any way? Check the box if your answer is yes.

   ☐ bedroom   ☐ yard   ☐ street   ☐ highway
   ☐ kitchen   ☐ school   ☐ park   ☐ parking lot

   ☐ other Please explain. _____

   _____

   _____

2. Do you make an effort to be kind to all living things? Check the box if your answer is yes for that item.

   ☐ parents   ☐ teachers   ☐ pets   ☐ mammals
   ☐ brothers   ☐ classmates   ☐ insects   ☐ reptiles
   ☐ sisters   ☐ friends   ☐ spiders   ☐ plants

   ☐ other Please explain. _____

   _____

   _____

3. Are you likely to become a smoker? _____

4. Are you likely to become a drug user? _____

5. Do you get in fights with other people? Check the truth.
   ☐ often   ☐ sometimes   ☐ rarely   ☐ never

6. Explain how you would solve a problem with another citizen in this world. _____

   _____

For official use only

Name of applicant: _____

☐ Citizenship granted   Official's signature: _____

☐ Citizenship denied   Date: _____

Rules of Conduct

Rules of Conduct

The inhabitants of

_____

do solemnly decree that the rules of conduct inscribed below must be dutifully followed to maintain citizenship in our world.

Idea List

The following list of ideas has been formulated to help the inhabitants of our new world embrace the ideas that help our world stay peaceful, and reject the ideas that may lead to our world's destruction.

IDEAS IN A NEW WORLD	
Ideas to embrace and promote	Ideas to reject and eliminate
idea: water conservation **reason:** Water is not always plentiful. It must be saved when it can be. **idea:** bicycling **reason:** _____ _____ _____	**idea:** air pollution **reason:** It is not good to breathe air into our bodies that is polluted. It hurts our lungs. **idea:** guns **reason:** _____ _____ _____
idea: **reason:** _____ _____ _____	**idea:** **reason:** _____ _____ _____
idea: **reason:** _____ _____ _____	**idea:** **reason:** _____ _____ _____
idea: **reason:** _____ _____ _____	**idea:** **reason:** _____ _____ _____
idea: **reason:** _____ _____ _____	**idea:** **reason:** _____ _____ _____
idea: **reason:** _____ _____	**idea:** **reason:** _____ _____

Bill Peet Books

Bill Peet has written and illustrated many, many books that have delighted people of all ages.

Look at these titles of books Bill Peet has written and illustrated.
Color the books you have read.
If you're a Bill Peet book lover, read as many of his books as you can.
Color the books you have finished on this reading record!

NO MATTER HOW HARD YOU TRY, THAT HISTORY BOOK DOESN'T HOLD YOUR INTEREST. ENTER THE PAST THROUGH ONE OF THESE BOOKS!

Ben and Me

by Robert Lawson

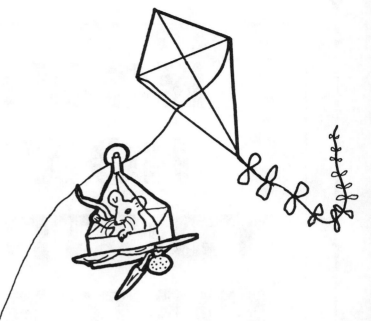

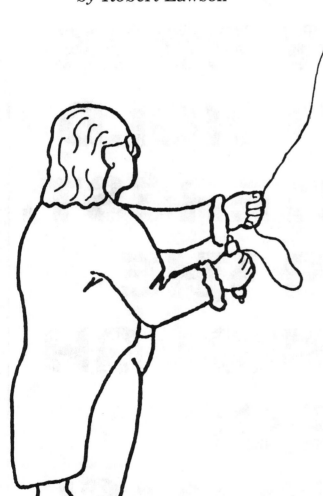

Benjamin Franklin led an interesting and useful life. As a printer, writer, editor, and publisher, he reached many people throughout the country and the world. His inventions made life easier and safer for others. His scientific discoveries opened new worlds of knowledge about the nature of electricity. As a statesman and diplomat, Franklin was a major factor in the United States' victory in the Revolutionary War. His was a many faceted life, full of excitement.

But, according to Robert Lawson, he did not accomplish all of his great achievements alone. In *Ben and Me,* we discover that a mouse named Amos played an instrumental part in Franklin's success.

You will be surprised by all Amos helped him do.

The *Real* Ben Franklin

Benjamin Franklin was a real person in American history. He did many, many things, and what he did, he did well. However, in *Ben and Me,* Amos takes quite a bit of credit for those things Franklin is said to have done.

What exactly **did** Ben Franklin do? Work with a partner, small group, or a class to research for facts about this great American. Include the following areas in your research.

Franklin's career as:

* a printer   * an inventor

* an editor   * a scientist

* an author   * a statesman

* a publisher   * a diplomat

Franklin's part in the following

things Amos mentions:

* the Franklin stove

* the Volunteer Fire Brigade

* *Poor Richard's Almanack*

* electricity

* the lightning rod

* lightning's relationship to electricity

* the famous kite experiment

* the trip to England on behalf of the colonists

* The Declaration of Independence

* the trip to France to raise funds for the Revolution

* a special relationship with a mouse

From Another Point of View . . .

In *Ben and Me,* we learn about Ben Franklin from another point of view. From Amos, we gain an entirely different perspective of a man so important in American history.

Can you imagine the story Red could tell about the life of Thomas Jefferson? Do you think other mice, rats, dogs, cats, birds, horses, or other animal companions might give us new insights into the lives of their famous masters?

What great men and women in history would you enjoy reading about from the point of view of an animal companion? Write three of your choices here.

1. _____

2. _____

3. _____

You will find the names of other great men and women in history on page 73.

Abraham Lincoln and his loyal dog

Irving Berlin with his faithful cat

This, of course, is just a partial list! Read this list and the list you have made. Choose one person for whom you know or can find historical information.

Write your choice here.

_____

It will be your job to rewrite a portion of this person's history from the point of view of an animal companion. Have fun and share your finished story with the class.

From Another Point of View . . .

Here is a partial list of great men and women in history. Before duplicating this list for your students, add the names of national or local famous people who have not been included in this list, but are of interest to your students.

SOME GREAT PEOPLE IN HISTORY

Walt Disney	Alexander Graham Bell	Abraham Lincoln
Babe Ruth	Nicholas Copernicus	Samantha Smith
Marie Curie	William Shakespeare	Neil Armstrong
John Muir	George Washington Carver	Frederick Douglass
Jesse Owens	Jacques Ives Cousteau	Galileo Galilei
Golda Meir	Babe Didrikson	Albert Einstein
Henry Ford	Wolfgang Amadeus Mozart	Harriet Tubman
Will Rogers	Franklin Delano Roosevelt	Mahatma Gandhi
Clara Barton	Martin Lurther King, Jr.	Roberto Clemente
Chief Joseph	Christopher Columbus	Johnny Appleseed
Mark Twain	Leonardo daVinci	Steven Spielberg
Irving Berlin	Thomas Alva Edison	Grandma Moses
Lee Trevino	Susan B. Anthony	Charles Lindbergh
Sacajawea	Florence Nightingale	Billie Jean King
Ryan White	Michelangelo Buonarroti	George Eastman
Bill Cosby	Laura Ingalls Wilder	Norman Rockwell
Sally Ride	Frank Lloyd Wright	Amelia Earhart
Jim Henson	Eleanor Roosevelt	Thomas Jefferson
Sammy Lee	Margaret Thatcher	Junipero Serra
Shirley Temple	Ella Fitzgerald	Cesar Chavez
Pocahontas	George Washington	Rachel Carson
Helen Keller	Margaret Mead	Jackie Robinson
Elvis Presley	Orville and Wilbur Wright	The Beatles
Louis Pasteur	John F. Kennedy	Jane Addams
W.E.B. DuBois	Wilma Rudolph	Sitting Bull
Ralph Nader	Davy Crockett	Robert Frost
Langston Hughes	Jim Thorpe	Bob Hope
Mother Teresa	Louisa May Alcott	Paul Revere

Runaway to Freedom

by Barbara Smucker

There was a time in the United States when men, women, and children who had black skin were treated like animals and forced to work long, hard hours for white-skinned masters. Many of these slaves were torn apart from their families, beaten unmercifully, and left with little hope for their futures.

But, rumors of a free land began to rekindle a feeling of hope among the slaves. "Canada — go to Canada. Follow the North Star to Canada, and there you will find freedom." The thought gave them strength to pursue that hope.

Runaway to Freedom is the story of two teen-age girls and their dangerous flight to freedom along the path of the Underground Railroad. It is also a story of the brave Abolitionists who helped them succeed in their journey.

The Way It Was

Julilly and Liza aren't quite sure what the Underground Railway is, even as they "ride" upon it. Jeb and Ella Brown explain it to the girls.

> "You don't know 'bout the railway? The slave catchers gave us the name. They said runaway slaves just seem to disappear underground and that there must be a railway down there."
>
> "We Abolitionists use the railway all the time. Coloured and white folks work together on it. Our homes, where we hide you slaves, are the 'railway stations.' The roads you all follow are the 'tracks.' You runaway slaves are the 'freight.' The women are 'dry goods' and the men are 'hardware.' "

Work as a class or in small groups to find out more about the Underground Railway.

*   Discover the origin of the Underground Railway.

*   Locate the North Star.

*   Examine the lives of famous Railroad conductors, such as Harriet Tubman, Alexander M. Ross, and Levi Coffin.

*   Trace the route followed by Julilly and Liza from the Riley Plantation in Mississippi to St. Catharines in Canada.

*   Find out the dangers the Abolitionists faced for helping slaves escape.

*   Understand the issues that separated slave holders from Abolitionists.

*   Include other research ideas of your own.

If You Were There . . .

Suppose you were alive during the time when slaves were bought and sold in the United States, and some of the lucky ones escaped to freedom on the Underground Railroad. Imagine some of the conversations you might hear!

Written below and on page 77 are ideas for creating conversations between characters in *Runaway to Freedom.* Cut out the idea cards and choose one or more that interest you. Work with a partner to create the dialogue that might have occured between the characters named on the cards in the given situations. When you have finished, perform your dialogue for the class.

Massa and Missy Hensen explain to their slaves how they feel about having to sell them to the slave traders.	Mammy Sally says her goodbyes to June Lilly as her daughter is sold into the hands of the slave traders.	Sims, the slave buyer, justifies why he has chosen June Lilly, Willie, Lester, Adam, and Ben.
Julilly asks Sims why he didn't get the slave children water on the long, dry trip to the deep South.	Hensen's overseer talks with Riley's overseer about techniques that really work with slaves.	Massa and Missy Riley come to the slave quarters and watch the children eat out of a trough.
Liza and Julilly make a list of things they will do when they are free.	Willie talks to Grannie about his mother. Grannie advises him what to do.	Liza tells Julilly the story of her attempt to escape and her recapture.

If You Were There . . . (cont.)

Here are more dialogue idea cards to cut and use. These cards could be put in a learning center area to be used during free exploration time or for special credit. Encourage your students to create dialogues for more than one card!

Alexander Ross talks to Lester and Adam about the Underground Railroad and their chance for freedom.	Lester and Adam try to convince Ben to escape with them. Ben makes his reasons clear.	The slave catchers celebrate their capture of Lester and Adam.
Alexander Ross tells Levi Coffin the story of how he was put into prison in Columbus, Mississippi.	Sheriff Starkey comes back to Levi Coffin's home later that same night. He has some words with Coffin about slavery.	Old Joe, the slave in Lexington, Kentucky, tells the other slaves on his plantation about the runaway "boys" he met.
Julilly and Liza talk to each other about how it feels to be really clean and have new clothes.	The Mennonite women talk to each other about Julilly and Liza.	Jeb Brown, Levi Coffin, Alexander Ross, and the Captain discuss the joys and dangers of their Abolitionist work.
Adam and Lester share their feelings as they stand on Canadian soil.	Mammy Sally tells Julilly and Liza about her escape to Canada.	Mammy Sally, Julilly, and Liza make plans for their future of freedom together.

Will You Sign Here, John Hancock?

by Jean Fritz

What do you know about John Hancock?

For most people what is remembered about this man of Colonial America is his name and the way he signed it. He is the signer of the Declaration of Independence who signed his name large enough for King George III to see it without his glasses!

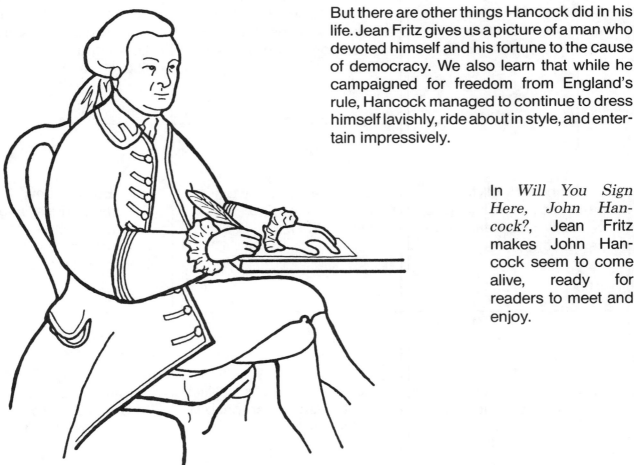

But there are other things Hancock did in his life. Jean Fritz gives us a picture of a man who devoted himself and his fortune to the cause of democracy. We also learn that while he campaigned for freedom from England's rule, Hancock managed to continue to dress himself lavishly, ride about in style, and entertain impressively.

In *Will You Sign Here, John Hancock?*, Jean Fritz makes John Hancock seem to come alive, ready for readers to meet and enjoy.

Together at Last!

Jean Fritz makes the relationship that existed between King George III and John Hancock very clear.

Why did King George III dislike John Hancock so much?

_____

_____

Why did John Hancock dislike King George III so much?

_____

_____

What was the "Dangerous Americans" list?

_____

_____

Suppose King George III and John Hancock were to meet in England. Work with a partner to create the dialogue that might have occured between them, as well as any action that might have happened as they talked.

Suppose John Hancock and King George III were to meet in Massachusetts. Work with a partner to create the dialogue that might have occured between them, as well as any action that might have happened as they talked.

* * * * *

Perform either or both of your dialogues and action ideas for the class.

Luck of the Draw!

Cut apart the task cards on this page and page 81. Put the cards face down on a table in front of the classroom. Divide the class in groups of three or four. Ask each group for a representative to choose a task card for the group. Then, allow each group time to complete the assigned tasks.

King George III placed John Hancock's name on the top of the "Dangerous Americans" list and a price of 500 pounds on his head.

Compute how much 500 pounds is in the money you use.

John Hancock once had to use a pewter teaspoon instead of a silver one. He once had to put out his candle with scissors instead of a snuffer.

Give John Hancock a true idea of what it might have been like to "Ruff It" in the Revolutionary War.

In the Common near John Hancock's house was a wishing stone. If you ran around it nine times and stood on it, you could make a wish.

Choose a "wishing object" and make up the rules that govern its use.

John Hancock loved to listen to the jokes of a hatter named Balch as he drove around Boston.

Prepare a group of "classroom-tellable" jokes for a John Hancock "Laugh-Off" Day!

Luck of the Draw! (cont.)

Cut apart the task cards on this page and combine them with the cards found on page 80.

John Hancock liked to be noticed.

Design the clothes that would get John Hancock noticed if he were to appear in your town today.

You may even want to plan a John Hancock fashion show!

The Stamp Act of 1765 imposed taxes on American colonists in 55 different ways.

Think of 55 ways to be taxed.

John Hancock was famous for his signature.

Practice writing John Hancock's name in his style of writing.

Plan a John Hancock look-alike signature contest.

John Hancock had nine "vehicles" in which he could ride about. They were all bright yellow.

Draw nine vehicles in which John Hancock would be proud to drive in the United States today.

Enter the Past!

Work as a class to make a reading card file on books about history and historical events that are fun to read! Each student will contribute at least one book choice for the card file. He or she must read the book first to make sure it's a good one!

Here are some card forms you can use for this file. Duplicate them on heavy paper and cut them apart.

Book Title: _____

_____

Author: _____

Time in history or historical event or person:

_____

_____

Person making recommendation:

_____

_____

Reasons for recommendation:
(see the back of this card.)

Book Title: _____

_____

Author: _____

Time in history or historical event or person:

_____

_____

Person making recommendation:

_____

_____

Reasons for recommendation:
(see the back of this card.)

Book Title: _____

_____

Author: _____

Time in history or historical event or person:

_____

_____

Person making recommendation:

_____

_____

Reasons for recommendation:
(see the back of this card.)

Book Title: _____

_____

Author: _____

Time in history or historical event or person:

_____

_____

Person making recommendation:

_____

_____

Reasons for recommendation:
(see the back of this card.)

ARE THERE THINGS ABOUT LIFE THAT ARE SOMETIMES HARD FOR YOU TO UNDERSTAND? BOOKS CAN HELP!

Annie
and the
Old One

by Miska Miles

Can you hold back time when you know someone you love deeply is near death? Annie thinks she can for her dear grandmother, the Old One.

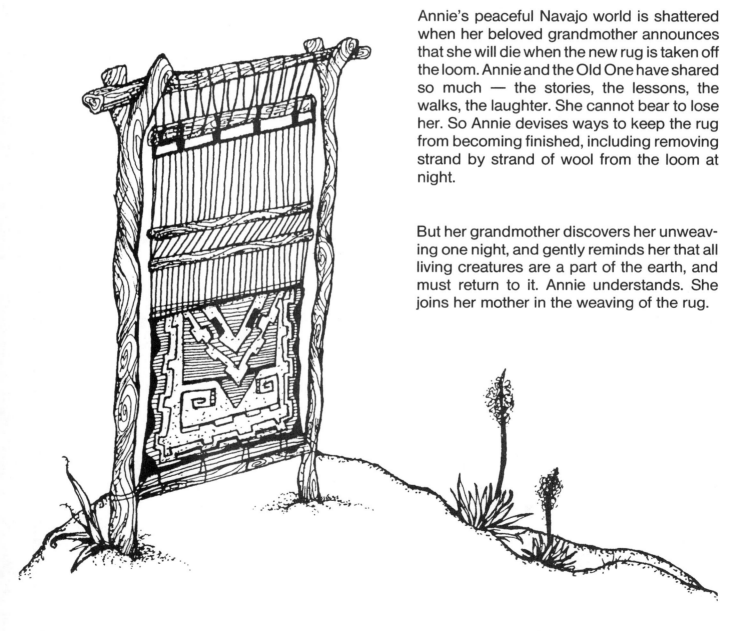

Annie's peaceful Navajo world is shattered when her beloved grandmother announces that she will die when the new rug is taken off the loom. Annie and the Old One have shared so much — the stories, the lessons, the walks, the laughter. She cannot bear to lose her. So Annie devises ways to keep the rug from becoming finished, including removing strand by strand of wool from the loom at night.

But her grandmother discovers her unweaving one night, and gently reminds her that all living creatures are a part of the earth, and must return to it. Annie understands. She joins her mother in the weaving of the rug.

Stopping the Movement of Time

There are moments in our lives we would like to hold onto forever. Annie wanted to hold her grandmother in life, even though the Old One was ready to die.

Suppose you could stop the movement of time to hold onto three very special moments in your life.

* What moments would you freeze?

* For how long would you want these moments frozen?

* Would the other people involved in your choice want to have this moment stopped for them as well?

* What would change in your life if this moment didn't move?

* What if the moments you've chosen could only be frozen for 24 hours. Would you still want them stopped?

Write the three special moments you would like to keep in the stopwatch. Choose one or more of these moments to write about, using some of the above questions to guide your writing.

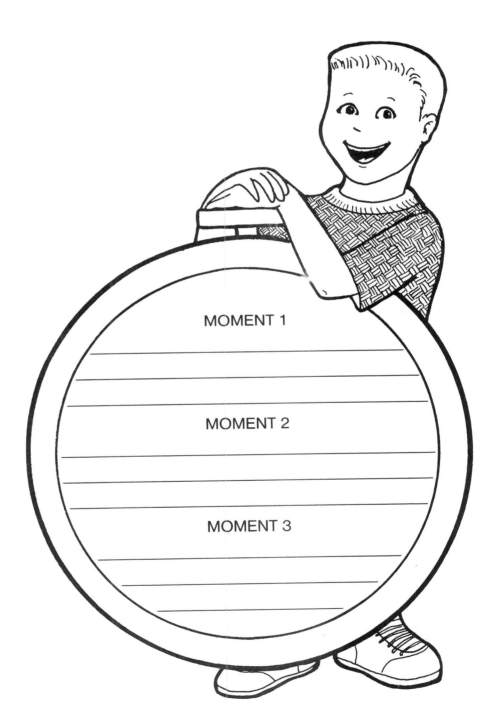

MOMENT 1

_____

_____

MOMENT 2

_____

_____

MOMENT 3

_____

_____

　　　85

Time To Weave!

You can learn some simple weaving techniques and create woven things just like the Navajo people!

Here are directions for weaving squares made on a cardboard loom.

1. Cut a piece of smooth cardboard into an almost square shape. Make the length of the cardboard 1 inch longer than its width.

2. 1/2 inch from each edge, draw a line across the top and bottom of the length ends.

3. Carefully cut slits up to the lines in each length end. The slits should be 1/4 inch apart. Be sure that you have the same number of slits at both the top and the bottom of your loom.

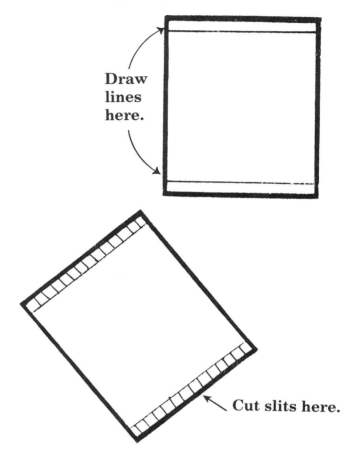

Draw lines here.

Cut slits here.

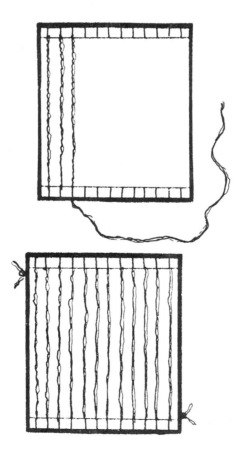

4. Knot a long piece of yarn at the end. Put the knot behind the top left slit.

5. Bring the yarn straight down to the bottom left slit. Wrap it under the flap of cardboard and come up to the second bottom slit from the left.

6. Bring the yarn straight up to the second top slit from the left. Go under and come up in the third slit.

7. Repeat this until you have come to the last slit. Knot the yarn behind it. These yarn strands are called the **warp.** Be sure they are not too tight. Otherwise your cardboard loom will bend!

Time To Weave! (cont.)

Continue weaving on your cardboard loom.

9. Drill a hole into the end of an ice cream stick. Use this stick like a needle. Thread it with another color of yarn. Make the length of yarn workable! You can always tie on another piece of yarn.

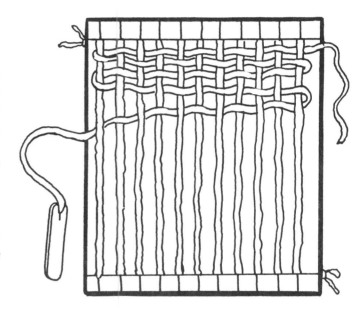

10. Weave across the warp, going over, then under. The yarn you are weaving with now makes the **weft.** When you are ready to go back across the warp, go over the strands you went under before. Push the weft strands closely together. Tie the weft strand where you began into a knot around the first warp strand.

11. Experiment with different colors of yarn for the weft. You will be able to create many interesting designs.

12. Completely fill the loom with the weft. Knot the end of the yarn under the last weave.

13. Carefully slip your weaving off of your cardboard loom.

Use your woven square for a potholder, placemat, or miniature blanket.

You may even want to stitch squares together to create larger things, such as blankets and rugs!

A Taste of Blackberries

by
Doris Buchanan Smith

To have a best friend is a very special thing. Two friends can share so much — silly times, adventures, secrets, laughter, sorrow, and especially love.

There is a rich friendship between Jamie and the narrator of *A Taste of Blackberries.* Not only are the two boys neighbors, but also best friends who spend as much of their lives as they can together, foraging through the woods for blackberries by day, sending messages across the street by Morse Code with flashlights by night.

However, Jamie is a trickster, fond of faking pains and injustices. So when he lies writhing in pain after being chased by bees, his best friend supposes he is faking his pain, as always. But, he is not. An allergic reaction to a bee sting causes his death.

The death of his best friend is hard for the narrator to accept and he experiences intense feelings of guilt and loss. But he realizes that Jamie would have wanted him to go on with his life, smiling and laughing, enjoying all he can from each day.

So with two baskets in hand, one for Jamie's mother and one for himself, the narrator rejoins his friend in the woods, remembering their joy while searching for a taste of blackberries.

The Accident

A Taste of Blackberries is told from a first person point of view. Jamie's best friend is the narrator, and we learn only what he thinks and feels. The story would have been different if another character in the story had told it.

You will work in groups to prepare a retelling of Jamie's death from the point of view of each of the characters in the box. Each group will be assigned one character from whose view the story will be told.

Jamie	Heather
Mrs. Houser	Jamie's Mother
Martha	The Paramedic
Mrs. Mullins	The Bees

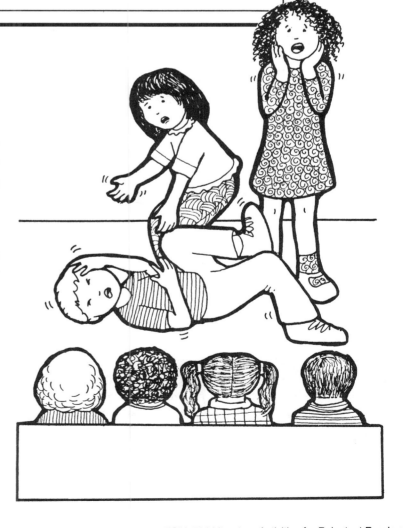

In your groups practice your point of view retelling. When you have perfected your story, prepare to dramatize it for the class.

Invite critiques from the class on the content of your story as well as your presentation.

A Taste of Blackberries ...

The narrator of the story finds an emotional link to his friend Jamie in the picking and tasting of blackberries. After Jamie's death, blackberries become a way for Jamie's young friend to ease his pain.

"Suddenly I thought about blackberries. They'd be ripe now. It seemed important to pick blackberries."

"I wanted to go blackberry picking with Jamie."

"I carried on a running conversation with myself, the berries, and sometimes with Jamie."

"Do you remember, I asked Jamie in my mind, the taste of blackberries?"

For the narrator, blackberries brought back fond memories of his dead friend. Blackberries also become a way for him to reach out to Jamie's mother. For both of them, a taste of blackberries will always bring Jamie back.

Sometimes, when we experience the death of a loved one, certain sights, sounds, smells, tastes, or touches will bring this person vividly to life in our minds. Is there a special thing that triggers the memory of someone who has died in your mind?

_____

_____

_____

_____

_____

The narrator of the story will be collecting blackberries throughout the season.

Help him find ways that he can use them and enjoy the memories of his friend Jamie while he does. Check page 91 for ideas.

A Taste of Blackberries ...

How many ways can you find to use blackberries? Write some of your ideas here.

Try some of the recipes and art projects that can be made with blackberries. Here are two examples for you to try.

BLACKBERRY COBBLER

Filling
2/3 cup sugar
2 tablespoons
   all-purpose flour
4 cups (1 pound)
   blackberries

Crust
1/2 cup all-purpose flour
1 teaspoon baking powder
1/2 cup whole-wheat flour

1½ tablespoons butter or
   margarine (chilled)
6 tablespoons milk

Preheat oven to 425°. Combine sugar and 2 tablespoons of flour in a medium-sized mixing bowl. Gently toss in berries. Pour the mixture into a 9-inch square baking dish. Prepare the crust according to the directions below. Put crust dough over berry mixture. Cut a few inch-long slits in crust dough to let steam escape. Bake for about 30 minutes until crust is browned. Serves six. (Increase recipe amounts to feed your class!)

Crust
In a small bowl, mix flours and baking powder. Cut in butter until mixture looks like coarse crumbs. Stir in milk and form a soft dough, and turn it out onto a lightly floured board. Knead lightly until dough is smooth. Roll it out to a square to cover the baking dish.

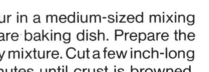

Try making art projects with blackberry stain. Be sure to wear old clothes!

Stone Fox

by
John Reynolds Gardiner

Little Willy lives with his grandfather on a potato farm in Wyoming. His grandfather has kept a secret from Willy — ten years of unpaid back taxes. Because he fears losing the farm to the $500 debt, Grandfather loses his will to live.

But Willy shoulders the responsibility of caring for his grandfather and the farm, and devises a way to make the money to pay the taxes. Little Willy enters the National Dogsled Race for a prize purse of $500, and is set to win with his faithful dog, Searchlight, pulling the sled.

However, the boy does not anticipate the formidable opponent he has in Stone Fox, the Shoshone Indian who has never lost a race. During the ten mile race, little Willy leads until 100 feet from the finish line, when Searchlight has a heart attack and dies. Touched by the boy and the dog's will to win, Stone Fox keeps the other race contestants from the finish line as little Willy carries Searchlight over to win the race.

"Go, Go, Go!"

Willy and Searchlight raced as fast as they could in the National Dogsled Races. The crowd was eager for Willy to win.

Conduct your own sled races! Design a sled using the basic sled pattern on this page, glue, colored pencils, two popsicle sticks, and three paper clips. Here's how.

diagram

1. Cut all the solid lines on the sled pattern; fold up all dashed lines.

2. Customize your sled with your own color choices. Be sure your designs will show when your sled has been folded and glued in place.

3. Glue TAB A to SIDE A and TAB B to SIDE B. Then glue TABS C and D to SIDE C.

4. Curl the long side around a pencil to form the front of the sled.

5. Glue a popsicle stick on the edge of each side for runners. (See diagram.)

6. Tape two sheets of poster board together; attach to the wall to make a sled run.

7. Each student will estimate the time his or her sled will take to race the course under the following conditions:
    *   no riders (empty sled)
    *   1 rider (1 paper clip attached in sled with tape)
    *   2 riders (2 attached paper clips)
    *   3 riders (3 attached paper clips)

8. Begin to race, using a stopwatch to keep track of actual time. Compare estimated and actual times.

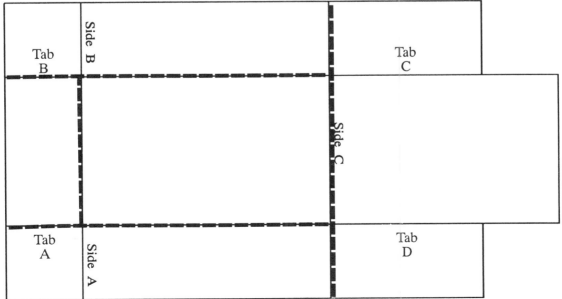

"Goodbye, Searchlight."

Willy and Searchlight were great companions and friends. When she died, a very important part of Willy's life died with her.

The readers of *Stone Fox* do not know what happens in Willy's life after he carries Searchlight over the finish line. We know Willy will do something for his dog.

Suppose Willy were to plan a special memorial service to honor his faithful companion. Help him organize it.

"Goodbye, Searchlight."

Time and date of memorial service: _____

Location of memorial service: _____

_____

Special guests to be invited: _____

_____

_____

Program: _____

_____

_____

_____

_____

_____

_____

Special words from

Willy: _____

_____

_____

Grandfather: _____

_____

_____

Stone Fox: _____

_____

"I Love You."

Books That Help Me Understand

These are some books I have read that have helped me understand things about life.

Book: _____

    Author: _____

    How it helped: _____

_____

Book: _____

    Author: _____

    How it helped: _____

_____

Book: _____

    Author: _____

    How it helped: _____

_____

Book: _____

    Author: _____

    How it helped: _____

_____

_____

_____

I'd like to share these books with my friends. The books will probably help them, too.

IF A BOOK IS GOOD, IT WILL HOLD YOUR INTEREST. TRY ONE OF THESE!

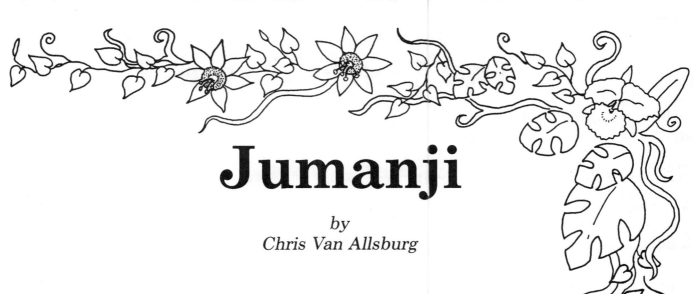

Jumanji

by
Chris Van Allsburg

While their parents were gone one afternoon, Judy and Peter found a long, thin box in the park across the street. It was a game: *Jumanji - A Jungle Adventure.* A note fastened to the box warned them to **read the directions carefully.** The children rushed home, eager to play the game.

It was like no game they had **ever** played before. When Peter landed on the square marked "Lion attacks," a lion appeared in the room, ready to charge. Soon, there were monkeys in the kitchen, monsoon rains in the living room, a rhinoceros stampede through the house, a python curled on the mantle, and other terrifying realities. As the volcano began to send hot lava out of the fireplace, Judy finished the game and yelled, "Jumanji!" The jungle and its dangers disappeared.

They quickly packed the game back into its box and returned it to the park, ready for the next children to find.

And two more children did find the game — Danny and Walter Budwing, who don't read instructions —ever.

 TCM-354 Literature Activities for Reluctant Readers

The Board Game

Peter and Judy find a very unusual board game in the park. This game gives them an afternoon of frightening excitement.

Do you play board games? _____

What are some of your favorite ones?

_____

_____

_____

_____

What do you like about board games?

_____

_____

Work with a partner to make a board game of your own. After your game is finished, trade and play with the games of the other students in your class. Be sure to read the directions carefully!

> ## Here is what you will need.

- an idea for a game that is fun
- a name for your game
- directions and rules
- a game board (A game board pattern can be found on pages 99 and 100. You may use this board or make your own.)
- playing pieces
- dice or a spinner to show how many spaces a player can move.

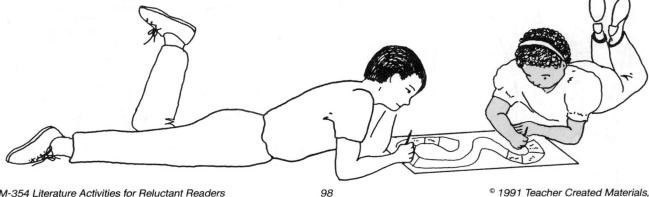

Jumanji

START HERE

Paste the left side of page 100 here.

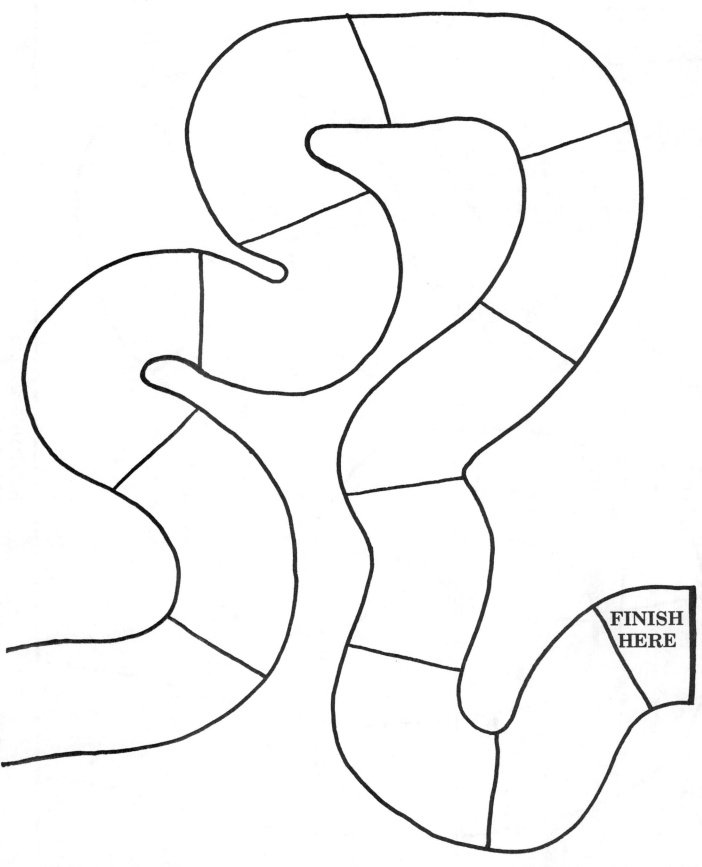

FINISH
HERE

It's Danny and Walter's Turn!

Peter and Judy play a jungle adventure game called *"Jumanji."* Because they carefully read the directions before they begin, the children are able to end the terrifying game before it's too late. They quickly return the game to the park where they found it.

However, from the window of their home, they see two boys they know running through the park with the game box. Peter and Judy know that Danny and Walter don't finish the games they start and **never** read directions.

Knowing what you know about the game of *"Jumanji"* and its rules, and what you have learned about Danny and Walter's game playing habits, create the story of Danny and Walter's experience with *"Jumanji: A Jungle Adventure Game."*

The Black Stallion

by
Walter Farley

On the return voyage from a two-month visit with his Uncle Ralph in India, Alec Ramsay thinks his journey home to Flushing, New York on the steamer *Drake* will be monotonous. Is he wrong!

From the moment the black stallion boards the *Drake,* the journey takes on new meaning for Alec. He is in awe of the mighty Black. But, a storm soon brings disaster to the ship and Alec frees the trapped horse from his stall. As the terrified animal plunges into the water, he accidently knocks Alec overboard. Fortunately, Alec manages to grab the Black's lead rope. With Alec hanging on, the Black swims to a tiny island. On the island they learn to depend on one another for survival and build a lasting bond of friendship. It is on the island that Alec learns to ride the Black.

Twenty days later they are rescued and Alec returns home with his new horse. With the help and encouragement of a knowledgeable ex-jockey, he trains the Black to apply his great speed on the race track. But, when they discover that the Black's lack of registration papers makes him ineligible to race, they devise a strategy to circumvent the rules. What they do captures the imagination of the entire country! An unofficial race with the greatest race horses of the day becomes the most exciting race of all time and leads Alec and the Black to the winner's circle in a triumph of friendship and love!

Alec and the Black

Alec and the Black share the joyful devotion and love that can sometimes develop between a person and an animal. They would each risk their lives to save the other, and do.

What draws Alec to the Black? _____

_____

_____

What draws the Black to Alec? _____

_____

_____

Describe how **you** felt as the relationship between the boy and the horse developed in the story.

_____

_____

_____

Suppose Alec and the Black were able to have a conversation that people could understand. Work in pairs to create the dialogues that might occur in each of these situations. When you are ready, perform your dialogues for the class.

Alec tells the Black how he felt about him the first time he saw him boarding the *Drake*. The Black shares how he felt when he was forced to get on the steamer.
The Black tells Alec how he felt when the boy grabbed his lead rope and held on until they reached the safety of the island. Alec tells how he felt, too.
Alec tells the Black how he felt to ride him. The Black tells Alec how it feels to be ridden by him.
The Black and Alec discuss their future together.

Think of some other situations involving Alec and the Black that you could dramatize. Write your ideas on the back of this paper.

Do You Want To Ride?

Read these sentences. Put a check mark in the box next to every sentence that is true for you.

☐ I wish I had a horse.

☐ I am afraid of horses.

☐ I like to read books about horses.

☐ I will never get on a horse.

☐ I love to watch horses run.

☐ I don't like the way horses smell.

☐ I sometimes pretend I am a horse.

☐ I like to draw horses.

☐ I have ridden a horse.

☐ I have fallen from a horse.

☐ I like horses.

☐ I would like to learn to ride a horse.

☐ I am wild about horses.

☐ I wish I were Alec Ramsey.

☐ I wish I were the Black.

When you read *The Black Stallion,* did you sometimes feel like you were riding the Black, just like Alec?

_____

Describe where you would ride and what you would feel if you were **really** riding the Black.

_____

_____

_____

_____

_____

_____

Hatchet

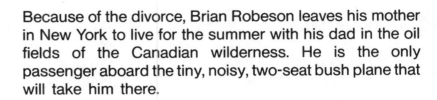

by
Gary Paulsen

Because of the divorce, Brian Robeson leaves his mother in New York to live for the summer with his dad in the oil fields of the Canadian wilderness. He is the only passenger aboard the tiny, noisy, two-seat bush plane that will take him there.

But while in the air, the pilot suffers a fatal heart attack, and 13-year-old Brian is left alone, 7000 feet above the ground somewhere over the northern wilderness.

The story of Brian Robeson's survival is a gripping and realistic one. Readers join him as he crash-lands in a lake, escaping with only the clothes he is wearing and a hatchet. We are with him as he combs the land for food, struggles to find a way to make fire, and is battered by a moose and a tornado. He soon realizes that **he** is all he has to survive.

Hatchet is a suspenseful story about the maturation of a boy in conditions that are extraordinary. It is written so we share the experience with him.

Survival

Here is a list of the things Brian had when he began his struggle for survival in the Canadian wilderness.

* a quarter	* a digital watch	* a hatchet
* three dimes	* a twenty dollar bill	* a belt
* a nickel	* a torn windbreaker	* a T-shirt
* two pennies	* odd pieces of paper	* socks
* a fingernail clipper	* underwear	* jeans
* a billfold	* tennis shoes	* himself

Which things on the list proved to be the most important?

_____

_____

Which things on the list proved to be worthless?

_____

_____

How would the story have been different if he had found the survival pack on the first day instead of the fifty-fourth?

_____

_____

_____

On the back of this paper, make a list of the things **you** would need to survive in the Canadian wilderness.

Brian Robeson In the News

Work in groups to create these events.

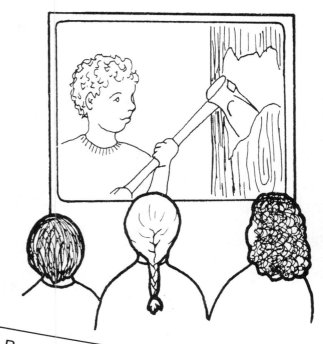

Reenact Brian's reunion with his mother and father in New York.

Plan Brian's presentation for a meeting about the wildlife in the Canadian wilderness.

Write the hospital report made on Brian's physical condition his first day back in town.

Broadcast the message the excited fur buyer sends on his plane's radio when he finds Brian Robeson alive!

Perform the conversation Brian has with Terry on a bike ride through a New York park.

Create a newspaper account of the Brian Robeson story!

Brian has been asked to make a commercial for hatchets. Write, direct, and perform this TV ad.

Write a letter to Jim or Jake's family about his heart attack.

From Brian's view, design a survival skills notebook to present to a scout meeting.

Create three recipes for the *Brian Robeson Survival Cookbook*.

Good Books Hold My Interest

These are some books that are the **best books** I have ever read.

Incentive Award

After your students have demonstrated their reading and enjoyment of books in a particularly memorable way, reward them with a choice from the class wish list!

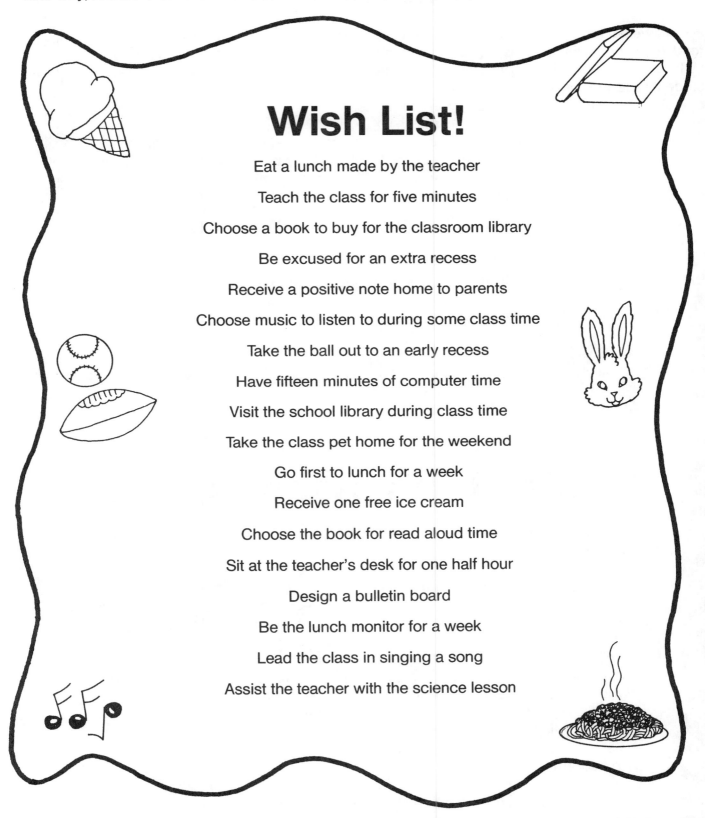

Wish List!

Eat a lunch made by the teacher

Teach the class for five minutes

Choose a book to buy for the classroom library

Be excused for an extra recess

Receive a positive note home to parents

Choose music to listen to during some class time

Take the ball out to an early recess

Have fifteen minutes of computer time

Visit the school library during class time

Take the class pet home for the weekend

Go first to lunch for a week

Receive one free ice cream

Choose the book for read aloud time

Sit at the teacher's desk for one half hour

Design a bulletin board

Be the lunch monitor for a week

Lead the class in singing a song

Assist the teacher with the science lesson

These are just a few wish list ideas. We're sure your students will have a few ideas of their own!

The Reading Chain

For six weeks (or so), encourage your students to complete a "link" for each book they read. Have them write their names and the names of each book and author on an 8½ by 1 inch strip of construction paper. Each strip is circled into a link and stapled or glued as all students attach their links together to make a chain. The chain grows in length on the wall or a class bulletin board as the six weeks progress.

At the end of the time period, all chains from the classroom (and other classrooms in the school and/or the district) can be attached to form a giant reading chain and displayed at a PTA meeting, an open house, a board meeting, or other important event!

Reward your students with a special day such as the one suggested below!

Celebrate Reading Day!

Help to create a schoolwide day where the focus is the celebration of reading. Here are some ideas.

* Invite an author to speak or read from his or her books.
* Recite poems.
* Have a book exchange.
* Arrange a young authors' showcase of books written and published by your school or class members.
* Invite the principal to read a favorite selection.
* Select a part from a favorite book to perform.
* Make books.
* Read stories to younger children.
* List the names of favorite books.
* Write or speak about why reading is important to you.
* Create lists of books that haven't been written, but you would read because of the title.
* Read!

Be sure to publicize this event. The community will appreciate positive news about education!

Answer Key

p.12

1. Alex blames his cat for the spilled food mess, and when he discovers that his cat has been gone and could not have possibly spilled the cat food, he blames one of his cat's friends.
2. He sneezes into Peter's collection and fuzz flies all over.
3. Alex tells Miss Henderson that his mother is a land turtle and she won Alex a baseball award, the Player with the Slowest Mother.
4. Alex burps into the microphone.
5. Alex thinks that planning to bunt means you have to vomit.
6. Alex tells T.J. that they shouldn't be that close unless they are dancing.
7. Alex pretends to be sick to try to get out of the game. One thing he does while "sick" is to crawl on the kitchen floor and eat his cereal like a dog with his head in the bowl.
8. Alex wears a gorilla costume instead of a sheep's costume in the Christmas play.
9. Alex flings his arms wildly and screams "BOOGA BOOGA!" at the first baseman.
10. Alex twists his face toward Harold's to make it appear that Harold has kissed him.
11. Alex's favorite relative is his grandmother, Steve Garvey.
12. Alex ends the church hymns in "doo-da."

p. 41

Check as a class activity. Answers are easily located in the book.

p. 42

from the top:
soil, sedimentary rock, metamorphic rock, igneous rock

soil
definition: top layer of the Earth's crust
description: made of ground-up rock, mixed with clay, bits of dead leaves, sticks, and small pebbles
example: dirt!

p. 42 (continued)

sedimentary rock
definition: rocks made from hardened layers of dust, sand, seashells, and other sediment "settled" through time
description: layered-looking rocks, sometimes containing fossils
example: sandstone, shale, limestone

metamorphic rock
definition: rocks that have been changed from one kind into another by heat and pressure
description: much harder than sedimentary rock
example: marble, slate

igneous rock
definition: melted rock that has cooled and hardened
description: varies, depending on type of rock
example: granite, obsidian, pumice

p. 43

from the top:
crust: the outside of the Earth, a shell of hard rock and soil
outer core: liquid metal
inner core: solid metal, a ball larger than the moon
mantle: hot solid rock
melted rock: pockets of melted rock under the Earth's crust

p. 50

arrow-poison frog—skin
sea anemone—tentacles
puff adder—poison gland/fangs
scorpion—stinger at the end of his tail
death puffer—blood and organs
scorpion fish—spine

Answer Key (con't.)

p.55

1) gigantic ogre; faint-hearted horse; horrified
2) throttle the monster in a trice!; before tea time
3) dim-witted noodlehead!
4) a "huffing snuffling" noise echoed
5) horror and amazement; En garde!
6) Wheeeefle!; gleefully squealed; spied; great horned snout
7) snorting fiercely, just like a high-spirited steed; charging headlong back into the gloomy old woods.
8) whuffling and gruffling on; giant step
9) desperate lunge, one tremendous surge of horsepower; hauled
10) burst into horrible howls and screeches that could be heard all the way to Twickenham.

p. 59

1) ocean 2) anemones 3) rival 4) herring
5) roosting nearby 6) account 7) weather
8) badly bruised snout 9) wild foamy trip
10) "gloop!" 11) patched trouser knees
12) nickel

p. 63

* The Wumps live in a pristine, beautiful, gentle, unpolluted world. They are gentle, peace-loving creatures.
* The Pollutians live in a crazed, polluted environment. It's noisy, dirty, congested, and frantic. They are a fast-paced, selfish, abusing people.

p. 79

* John Hancock would not pay taxes to England. This greatly angered the King.
* John Hancock did not like the fact that King George could "reach all the way across the Atlantic Ocean and try to take money from his pocket." Hancock thought the taxes were unjust.
* The list of "Dangerous Americans" was one King George kept of colonists who were dangerous to England because they did not obey the rules of the "Mother" country to the King's satisfaction.

p. 106

most important: himself, hatchet, articles of clothing
worthless: money, paper